8882
8KU
BUZA

About the author

Tony Buzan, inventor of the now world-famous Mind Maps®, has
achieved an astonishing series of accomplishments.

- The world's leading author on the brain and learning (over 80 authored

Also by Tony Buzan

Books

The Mind Set:

    Use Your Head

    Master Your Memory

    The Speed Reading Book

    The Mind Map Book

Get Ahead

Brain S£11

Super Sell

BrainSmart Leader

Sales Genius

Mind Maps in Medicine

The Brain Book

Brain Training

Lessons from the Art of Juggling

Buzan's Book of Mental World Records

Man Versus Machine

*Synapsia (*Individual)

Synapsia (89–99 complete set)

The Younger Tongue

Brain Power for Kids

Teach Yourself Revision Guides
(GCSE level in 17 subjects)

Teach Yourself Revision Guides
(A level in 8 subjects)

Teach Yourself Literature Guides
(22 titles)

How to Mind Map

The Power of Spritual Intelligence

The Power of Social Intelligence

The Power of Verbal Intelligence

Head Strong

The Power of Creative Intelligence

Head First

Mind Maps for Kids

Video tapes

Learning with Lana

Developing Family Genius

Get Ahead

If at First . . .

Mindpower

Audio tapes

Use Your Head

Buzan On . . .

    The Brain

    Memory

    Thinking & Creativity

    Success

    Reading Mind & Body

    Mind Mapping

Mind Mapping Natural Genius

The Genius Formula

Brain S£ll

Other products

Brain Club – Home Study Plan

Body & Soul Poster (Limited Edition)

Desiderata Reconsidered

Universal Personal Organiser

Mind Map Kit

Software

Mind Manager (CD-ROM)

Mind Manager (Trial CD-ROM)

Mastering Memory
(Computer Software & Manual)

Use
Your Memory

Tony Buzan

Dedicated to Zeus
and Mnemosyne's ideal muse-
child: my dear, dear friend
Lorraine Gill, the Artist

External Editor-in-chief: Vanda North

Published by BBC Worldwide Limited,
Woodlands, 80 Wood Lane, London W12 OTT

First published in 1986
Revised and updated 1989, 1995
This revised edition published in 2003
Reprinted 2003

ISBN 0 563 48703 8

Mind Map ® is a registered trademark of the Buzan Organisation 1990
Mental Literacy ® is a registered trademark of the Buzan Organisation 1994
Radiant Thinking ® is a registered trademark of the Buzan Organisation 1994

Series design by Ben Cracknell Studios
Illustrations by Alan Burton and Ben Cracknell Studios

Commissioning Editor: Emma Shackleton
Project Editor: Cath Harries

Set in Meridien 9.75/12.5pt
Printed and bound in Great Britain by The Bath Press, Bath
Cover printed by Belmont Press Ltd, Northampton
Plate sections printed by Lawrence-Allen Ltd, Weston-super-Mare
Colour separations by Radstock Reproductions, Midsomer Norton, Somerset

Contents

Part Three Mind Maps® for Memory

Appreciation

With thanks to all those whose effort and co-operation enabled me to write this book:

Zita Albes; Jennie Allen; Astrid Andersen; Jeannie Beattie; Nick Beytes; Lesley Bias; Mark Brown; Joy Buttery; my brother, Barry Buzan; Bernard Chibnall; Tessa Clark; Carol Coaker; Steve and Fanny Colling; Susan Crockford; Tricia Date; Janet Dominey; Charles Elton; Janice English; Lorraine Gill; Bill Harris; Brian Helweg-Larsen; Thomas Jarlov; Trish Lillis; Hermione Lovell; Annette McGee; Joe McMahon; Vanda North; Dominic O'Brien; Khalid Ranjah; Pep Reiff; Auriol Roberts; Ian Rosenbloom; Caitrina Ni Shuilleabhain; Robert Millard Smith; Chris and Pat Stevens; Jan Streit; Christopher Tatham; Lee Taylor; Nancy Thomas; Sue Vaudin; Jim Ward; Bill Watts; Gillian Watts; Susan Whiting; Phyllida Wilson.

Foreword

This edition of *Use Your Memory* is in honour of the introduction through *Use Your Head* of Mind Maps to the global community in the spring of 1974. Mind Maps were the first new major memory systems to be introduced for five centuries.

To mark the dawn of the Century of the Brain and the Millennium of the Mind, the BBC launched **The Mind Set,** the first encyclopedia on the use of the brain, which features an updated version of the five essential Brain Books: *Use Your Head* and its 'children', *Use Your Memory, Master Your Memory, The Mind Map Book,* and *The Speed Reading Book.*

In the early 1990s so many people were becoming interested in the power of memory, that it was decided to hold the first Memoriad – World Memory Championship. Using the principles and techniques outlined in *Use Your Memory,* competitors were able to remember a deck of cards in under 3 minutes, numbers as long as 1000 digits, and various lists of data at incredible speeds.

Dominic O'Brien and Jonathan Hancock, both World Memory Champions, explained to the world how they build gigantic mental Memory Maps based on the principles of SMASHIN' SCOPE (*see page 45*). Success stories based on the application of the *Use Your Memory* principles and Mind Maps abound.

At Eton College, James Longworth, a 16-year-old student, established world student records for the memorisation of cards (1½ minutes for an entire pack!) as well as for the speed memorisation of numbers. Applying memory techniques and Mind Mapping to his studies, he has managed to achieve outstanding academic results, while maintaining an exceptionally active life in athletics, theatre, student activities and design.

Natasha Diot, of St. David's School, Ashford, Middlesex, became the Women's World Memory Champion, achieved nine A's in her GCSEs, was head girl for sports, and has become a research assistant for *Buzan's Book of Genius.*

And James Lee, memorist, has become a television star. He recently appeared on a programme in which he astounded viewers by performing amazing memory feats.

Inspired by such examples, members of the Use Your Head Clubs have formed a special subdivision – the 'Mnemons' who practise memory techniques both as 'mental aerobics' and as a method for memorising tens of thousands of units of information useful to them in their everyday lives.

In 1993, the principles outlined in *Use Your Memory*, and especially the theory behind the story of Zeus and Mnemosyne (*see page 48*) gave rise to the new mental formula $E + M = C^{\infty}$. This formula explains that if you put energy into your memory, it will lead to infinite creativity.

Your adventure into these magical and fantastic realms begins . . .

Introduction

Like so many children, as a youth I was mystified by the wonderful and elusive faculty called memory. In casual and relaxed situations it worked so smoothly that I hardly ever noticed it; in examinations it only occasionally performed well, to my surprise, but was more often associated with 'bad memory', the fearful area of forgetting. Since I spent much of my childhood in the country with animals, I began to realise that the misnamed 'dumb' creatures seemed to have extraordinary memories, often superior to my own. Why, then, was human memory apparently so faulty?

I began to study in earnest, eagerly devouring information about how the early Greeks had devised specific memory systems for various tasks; and how later, the Romans applied these techniques to enable themselves to remember whole books of mythology and to impress their audiences during senatorial speeches and debates. My interest became more focused while I was in college, when the realisation slowly dawned on me that such basic systems need not be used only for 'rote' or parrotlike memory, but could be used as gigantic filing systems for the mind, enabling extraordinarily fast and efficient access, and enormously enhancing general understanding. I applied the techniques in taking examinations, in playing games with my imagination in order to improve my memory, and in helping other students, who were supposedly on the road to academic failure, achieve first-class successes.

The explosion of brain research during the last decade has confirmed what the memory theorists, gamesters, mnemonic technicians and magicians have always known: that the holding capacity of our brains and the ability to recall what is stored there are far and deliciously beyond normal expectations.

Use Your Memory, a major new development from the memory sections of *Use Your Head*, is an initial tour through what should have been included as first among the seven wonders of the world: the 'hanging gardens' of your limitless memory and imagination.

How to Use *Use Your Memory*

Use Your Memory has been designed to enable you to achieve your memory goals as rapidly as possible.

It is divided into three main parts: Part I covers Memory History and Systems; Part II the Major System and its Application to Memory; and Part III the uses of Mind Maps for Memorising.

More specifically, chapters 1 to 9 provide you with a check of your current memory capabilities, with background information on your memory, including the foundations and principles you will require for developing a superpower memory. The first basic link and list systems for memorising 10, 20 and 26 items, are explained.

Chapter 10 then shows you how to multiply any system you have learnt by first a factor of ten, and then by a factor of ten again!

Chapter 11 introduces you to your memory's rhythms over time, enabling you to manage yourself and life in such a way as to increasingly enhance your memory's functioning.

Chapter 12 introduces you to the Major System. This system is so named because it forms the basis for a limitless series of other memory systems, and can be specifically applied to the memorisation of those areas dealt with in chapters 14 to 21: the memorisation of cards; the development of your IQ through long number memory; telephone numbers; schedules and appointments; dates in the twentieth century; historical dates; birthdays and anniversaries; and vocabulary and language learning.

Chapter 22 introduces you to the new technique of Mind Mapping, an approach to the art of memory that will allow you to note and record in a manner that will improve your retention and recall by as much as 10 times the average.

The Mind Mapping technique can be applied, with other memory systems and approaches, to the next five chapters (23 to 27) on the memorisation of names and faces, the recalling of things you thought you had forgotten, the writing and passing of examinations, the giving of speeches and telling of jokes, and the recalling of your dreams.

It is recommended that you browse through the whole book first, then complete chapters 1 to 13 to give yourself a solid foundation.

Having reached this stage, you may either continue through the book on a chapter-by-chapter basis, choosing any chapter from 14 to 21, or jump ahead to chapter 22 and subsequently pick your preferred choices from chapters 23 to 28.

Above all, make sure that as you progress through the book you use, to their fullest extent, your **associative** and **imaginative** abilities, and that you enjoy yourself!

Part One
Memory

Its History and Systems

Is Your Memory
Perfect?

1

Preview

- Shifting the negative mental set

> There is now increasing evidence that our memories may not only be far better than we ever thought but may in fact be perfect.

Your memory is phenomenal. This statement is made despite the following counterarguments:

1. Most people remember fewer than 10 per cent of the names of those whom they meet.
2. Most people forget more than 99 per cent of the phone numbers given to them.
3. Memory is supposed to decline rapidly with age.
4. Many people drink, and alcohol is reputed to destroy 1000 brain cells per drink.
5. Internationally, across races, cultures, ages and education levels, there is a common experience, and fear of, having an inadequate or bad memory.
6. Our failures in general, and especially in remembering, are attributed to the fact that we are 'only human', a statement that implies that our skills are inherently inadequate.
7. You will probably fail most of the memory tests in the following chapter.

Points 1, 2 and 7 will be dealt with through the remainder of the book. You will see that it is possible, with appropriate knowledge, to pass all the tests, and that names and phone numbers are easy to remember – if you know how.

There is no evidence to suggest that moderate drinking destroys brain cells. This misapprehension arose because it was found that excessive drinking, and only excessive drinking, did indeed damage the brain.

Brain Bites

Your memory may decline with age, but only if it is not used. Conversely, if it is used, it will continue to improve throughout your lifetime.

Across cultural and international boundaries 'negative experience' with memory can be traced not to our being 'only human' or in any way innately inadequate but to two simple, easily changeable factors: (1) negative mental set and (2) lack of knowledge.

Shifting the Negative Mental Set

There is a growing and informal international organisation, which I choose to name the 'I've Got an Increasingly Bad Memory Club'. How often do you hear people in animated and enthusiastic conversation saying things like, 'You know, my memory's not nearly as good as it used to be when I was younger; I'm constantly forgetting things.' To which there is an equally enthusiastic reply: 'Yes, I know exactly what you mean; the same thing's happening to me....' And off they dodder, arms draped around each other's shoulders, down the hill to mental oblivion. And such conversations often take place between 30-year-olds!

This negative, dangerous, *incorrect* mental set is based on lack of proper training, and this book is designed to correct it.

Consider the younger supermemoriser to whom most people romantically refer. If you want to check for yourself, go back to any school at the end of the day, walk into a classroom of a group of five to seven-year-old children after they have gone home and ask the teacher what has been left in the classroom (i.e. forgotten). You will find the following items: watches, pencils, pens, sweets, money, jackets, physical education equipment, books, coats, glasses, erasers, toys, etc.

The only real difference between the middle-aged executive who has forgotten to phone someone he was supposed to phone and who has left his briefcase at the office, and the seven-year-old child who realises on returning home that he's left at school his watch, his pocket-money and his homework, is that the seven-year-old does not collapse into depression, clutching his head and exclaiming, 'Oh God, I'm seven years old and my memory's going!'

Ask yourself, 'What is the number of things I actually remember each day?' Most people estimate somewhere between 100 and 10,000. The answer is in fact in the multiple billions. The human memory is so excellent and runs so smoothly that most people don't even realise that every word they speak and every word they listen to are instantaneously produced for consideration, recalled, recognised precisely and placed in their appropriate context. Nor do they realise that every moment, every perception, every thought, *everything* that they do throughout the entire day and throughout their lives is a function of their memories. In fact, its ongoing accuracy is almost perfect. The few odd things that we do forget are like odd specks on a gigantic ocean. Ironically, the reason why we notice so dramatically the errors that we make is that they are so rare.

There are various arguments to support the theory that our memories may be perfect:

1 ● Dreams
Many people have vivid dreams of acquaintances, friends, family and lovers of whom they have not thought for as many as 20 to 40 years. In their dreams, however, the images are *perfectly* clear, all colours and details being exactly as they were in real life. This confirms that somewhere in the brain there is a vast store of perfect images and associations that does not change with time and that, with the right trigger, can be recalled. In chapter 27 (*page 179*) you will learn about Catching Your Dreams.

2 ● Surprise Random Recall
Practically everyone has had the experience of turning a corner and suddenly recalling people or events from previous times in

his life. This often happens when people revisit their first school. A single smell, touch, sight or sound can bring back a flood of experiences thought to be forgotten. This ability of any given sense to reproduce perfect memory images, the fact that the smell of bread baking or the sound of a song can bathe your mind in the past, indicates that if there were more correct 'trigger situations' much more would and could be recollected. We know from such experiences that the brain has retained the information.

3 ● The Russian 'S' (Shereshevsky)

In the early part of this century a young Russian journalist, Shereshevsky (in *The Mind of a Mnemonist*, by A. R. Luria, he is referred to as 'S') attended an editorial meeting, and it was noted to the consternation of others that he was not taking notes. When pressed to explain, he became confused; to everyone's amazement, it became apparent that he really did not understand why anyone should ever take notes. The explanation that he gave for not taking notes himself was that he could remember what the editor was saying, so what was the point? Upon being challenged, 'S' reproduced the entire speech, word for word, sentence for sentence, and inflection for inflection. For the next 30 years he was to be tested and examined by Alexander Luria, Russia's leading psychologist and expert on memory. Luria confirmed that 'S' was in no way abnormal but that his memory was indeed perfect. Luria also stated that at a very young age 'S' had 'stumbled upon' the basic mnemonic principles (*see chapter 4, page 44*) and that they had become part of his natural functioning.

'S' was not unique. The history of education, medicine and psychology is dotted with similar cases of perfect memorisers. In every instance, their brains were found to be normal, and in every instance they had, as young children, 'discovered' the basic principles of their memory's function.

4 ● Professor Rosensweig's Experiments

Professor Mark Rosensweig, a Californian psychologist and neurophysiologist, spent years studying the individual brain cell and its capacity for storage. As early as 1974 he stated that if we fed in ten new items of information *every second* for an entire lifetime to any normal human brain that brain would be considerably less than half full. He emphasised that memory problems have nothing to do with the capacity of the brain but rather with the self-management of that apparently limitless capacity.

5 ● Professor Penfield's Experiments

Professor Wilder Penfield of Canada came across his discovery of the capacity of human memory by mistake. He was stimulating individual brain cells with tiny electrodes for the purpose of locating areas of the brain that were the cause of patients' epilepsy.

To his amazement he found that when he stimulated certain individual brain cells, his patients were suddenly recalling experiences from their past. The patients emphasised that it was not simple memory, but that they actually were reliving the entire experience, including smells, noises, colours, movement, tastes. These experiences ranged from a few hours before the experimental session to as much as 40 years earlier.

Penfield suggested that hidden within each brain cell or cluster of brain cells lies a perfect store of every event of our past and that if we could find the right stimulus we could replay the entire film.

6 ● The Potential Pattern-Making Ability of Your Brain

Professor Pyotr Anokhin, the famous Pavlov's brightest student, spent his last years investigating the potential pattern-making capabilities of the human brain. His findings were important for memory researchers. It seems that memory is recorded in separate little patterns, or electromagnetic circuits, that are formed by the brain's interconnecting cells.

Anokhin already knew that the brain contained a million million (1,000,000,000,000) brain cells but that even this gigantic number was going to be small in comparison with the number of patterns that those brain cells could make among themselves. Working with advanced electron microscopes and computers, he came up with a staggering number. Anokhin calculated that the number of patterns, or 'degrees of freedom', throughout the brain is, to use his own words, 'so great that writing it would take a line of figures, in normal manuscript characters, more than ten and a half million *kilometres* in length. With such a number of possibilities, the brain is a keyboard on which hundreds of millions of different melodies can be played.'

Your memory is the music.

7 ● Near-Death-Type Experiences

Many people have looked up at the surface ripples of a swimming pool from the bottom, knowing that they were going to drown within the next two minutes; or seen the rapidly disappearing ledge of the mountain from which they have just fallen; or felt the oncoming grid of the 10-ton lorry bearing down on them at 60 miles per hour. A common theme runs through the accounts that survivors of such traumas tell. In such moments of 'final consideration' the brain slows all things down to a standstill, expanding a fraction of a second into a lifetime, and reviews the total experience of the individual.

When pressed to admit that what they had really experienced were a few highlights, the individuals concerned insisted that what they had experienced was their *entire* life, including all things they had completely forgotten until that instant of time. 'My whole life flashed before me' has almost become a cliché that goes with the near-death experience. Such a commonality of experience again argues for a storage capacity of the brain that we have only just begun to tap.

8 ● Photographic Memory

Photographic, or eidetic, memory is a specific phenomenon in which people can remember, usually for a very short time, perfectly and exactly anything they have seen. This memory usually fades, but it can be so accurate as to enable somebody, after seeing a picture of 1000 randomly sprayed dots on a white sheet, to reproduce them perfectly. This suggests that in addition to the deep, long-term storage capacity, we also have a shorter-term and immediate photographic ability. It is argued that children often have this ability as a natural part of their mental functioning and that we train it away by forcing them to concentrate too much on logic and language and too little on imagination and their other range of mental skills.

9 ● The 1000 Photographs

In recent experiments people were shown 1000 photographs, one after the other, at a pace of about one photograph per second. The psychologists then mixed 100 photographs with the original 1000, and asked the people to select those they had not seen the first time through. Everyone, regardless of how he described his normal memory, was able to identify almost every photograph he had seen – as well as each one that he had not seen previously. They were not necessarily able to remember the order in which the photographs had been presented, but they could definitely remember the image – an example that confirms the common human experience of being better able to remember a face than the name attached to it. This particular problem is easily dealt with by applying the Memory Techniques.

10 ● The Memory Techniques

The Memory Techniques, or mnemonics, were a system of 'memory codes' that enabled people to remember perfectly whatever it was they wished to remember. Experiments with these techniques have shown that if a person scores 9 out of 10 when using such a technique, that same person will score 900 out of 1000, 9000 out of 10,000, 900,000 out of 1,000,000 and so on. Similarly, one who scores perfectly out of 10 will score perfectly out of 1,000,000. These techniques help us to delve into that phenomenal storage capacity we have and to pull out whatever it is that we need. The Memory Principles are outlined in chapter 4, and the bulk of this book is devoted to explaining and outlining the most important and useful of these systems, showing how easily they can be learned, and how they can be applied in personal, family, business and community life.

Onword

At this early stage it should be helpful for you to test your memory in its current state. The following chapter provides a series of memory tests that will form a foundation from which you can check your progress. If you are interested in the truth about yourself and your performance now, as compared with what it will be when you have completed the book, perform these tests thoroughly. Most people do rather poorly at the beginning, improving dramatically as they progress through the chapters.

Checking
Your Current Memory
Capabilities

2

> Few people ever put their memories to the immediate test, and it is for this reason that most are unaware of the false limits, the habits and potential of their minds.

Because of the way we are trained (or not trained) in school, the simple tasks you will soon attempt will in some cases prove very difficult and in others almost impossible. Yet these tasks are perfectly within the capacity of the average human brain. Do not worry about a potentially poor performance, however, since it is the purpose of this book to make memorisation, such as is required in the following tests, an easy and enjoyable exercise.

Link Test

Read the following list of twenty items through *once* only, trying to memorise both the items and the order in which they are listed. Then turn to page 28 to test yourself and for scoring instructions.

Wallpaper	Scissors	Power	Perfume
Mountain	Nail	Elephant	Safe

Skirt	Watch	Jail	Melon
String	Nurse	Mirror	Mongrel
Ice cream	Plant	Suitcase	Engraving

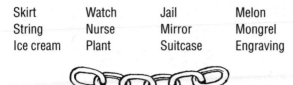

Peg Test

Give yourself sixty seconds to memorise the following list of 10 items. The aim in this test is to remember the items in random order, connecting them to their appropriate number. When your minute has passed, turn to page 28 and fill in the answers.

1 Atom	5 Alley	9 Brush
2 Tree	6 Tile	10 Toothpaste
3 Stethoscope	7 Windscreen	
4 Sofa	8 Honey	

Number Test

Look at the four 15-digit numbers printed below, giving not more than a half-minute to each. At the end of each half-minute section turn to page 29 and write down the number as best you can.

1 798465328185423   3 784319884385628
2 493875941254945   4 825496581198762

Telephone Number Test

The following is a list of ten people and their telephone numbers. Study the list for not more than two minutes and attempt to remember all the phone numbers, then turn to page 29 and answer the appropriate questions.

Your health-food shop	787-5953
Your tennis partner	640-7336
Your local weather bureau	691-0262
Your local newsagent	242-9111
Your local florist	725-8397
Your local garage	781-3702
Your local theatre	869-9521
Your local nightclub	644-1616
Your local community centre	457-8910
Your favourite restaurant	354-6350

Card Test

This test is designed to exercise your present capacity in remembering cards and their sequence. The list below contains all 52 cards of the regular pack in numbered order. Your task is to spend not more than five minutes looking at this list, and then to recall it. Turn to page 30 to fill in your answers.

1	Ten of diamonds	27	Four of hearts
2	Ace of spades	28	Two of diamonds
3	Three of hearts	29	Jack of spades
4	Jack of clubs	30	Six of spades
5	Five of clubs	31	Two of hearts
6	Five of hearts	32	Four of diamonds
7	Six of hearts	33	Three of spades
8	Eight of clubs	34	Eight of diamonds
9	Ace of clubs	35	Ace of hearts
10	Queen of clubs	36	Queen of spades
11	King of spades	37	Queen of diamonds
12	Ten of hearts	38	Six of diamonds
13	Six of clubs	39	Nine of spades
14	Three of diamonds	40	Ten of clubs
15	Four of spades	41	King of hearts
16	Four of clubs	42	Nine of hearts
17	Queen of hearts	43	Eight of spades
18	Five of spades	44	Seven of spades
19	Jack of diamonds	45	Three of clubs
20	Seven of hearts	46	Ace of diamonds
21	Nine of clubs	47	Ten of spades
22	King of diamonds	48	Eight of hearts
23	Seven of clubs	49	Seven of diamonds
24	Two of spades	50	Nine of diamonds
25	Jack of hearts	51	Two of clubs
26	King of clubs	52	Five of diamonds

Face Test

Look at the ten faces on pages 26–27 for not more than two minutes, then turn to pages 31 and 32 where the same faces are present without their names. Try to match the right name to the right face. Scoring instructions are on page 32.

Dates Test

This is your last test: listed below are ten fairly important historical dates. Give yourself two minutes to remember them all perfectly, then turn to page 33.

1 1666 Great Fire of London
2 1770 Beethoven's birthday
3 1215 Signing of Magna Carta
4 1917 Russian Revolution
5 1454 First printing press
6 1815 Battle of Waterloo
7 1608 Invention of the telescope
8 1905 Einstein's Theory of Relativity
9 1789 French Revolution
10 1776 American Declaration of Independence

1 Mrs Whitehead   2 Mr Hawkins

3 Mr Fisher

4 Mr Ramm   5 Mrs Hemming

6 Mrs Briar

7 Mr Chester

8 Mr Master

9 Mrs Swanson

10 Miss Temple

Link Test Response (*See p. 22*)

Note in the space provided all the items you can remember, in correct order.

_____
_____
_____
_____
_____
_____
_____
_____
_____
_____
_____
_____
_____

Score yourself in two ways: first enter below the number of items you remembered out of 20, and then record the number of items you listed in the correct order. (If you reversed two items, they are both wrong with regard to order.) Score one point for each remembered; one point for each correct placing (total possible: 40).

Number remembered: Number in correct order:
Number incorrect: Number in incorrect order:

Peg Test Response (*See p. 23*)

In the order indicated. place the item you were given next to its appropriate number.

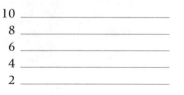

10 _____   1 _____
8 _____   3 _____
6 _____   5 _____
4 _____   7 _____
2 _____   9 _____

Number correct:

Number Test Response (*See p. 23*)

In the spaces below write down each of the four 15-digit numbers.

1 _____
2 _____
3 _____
4 _____

Score one point for every digit that you record *in its proper sequence.*

Total score: ____
           60

Telephone Number Test Response (*See p. 23*)

Write down, in the spaces provided, the phone numbers of the ten people.

Name	Number
1 Your health-food shop	_____
2 Your tennis partner	_____
3 Your local weather bureau	_____
4 Your local newsagent	_____
5 Your local florist	_____
6 Your local garage	_____
7 Your local theatre	_____
8 Your local nightclub	_____
9 Your local community centre	_____
10 Your favourite restaurant	_____

Scoring: give yourself one mark for each correct number (even if you make only one mistake in the number you must consider this totally wrong, for if you had dialled it you would not have been put in contact with the person with whom you wished to speak). The highest possible score is 10.

Score: ____
      10

Card Test Response (*See p. 24*)

Recall the list in reverse order (52–1) as indicated.

52 _____	26 _____
51 _____	25 _____
50 _____	24 _____
49 _____	23 _____
48 _____	22 _____
47 _____	21 _____
46 _____	20 _____
45 _____	19 _____
44 _____	18 _____
43 _____	17 _____
42 _____	16 _____
41 _____	15 _____
40 _____	14 _____
39 _____	13 _____
38 _____	12 _____
37 _____	11 _____
36 _____	10 _____
35 _____	9 _____
34 _____	8 _____
33 _____	7 _____
32 _____	6 _____
31 _____	5 _____
30 _____	4 _____
29 _____	3 _____
28 _____	2 _____
27 _____	1 _____

Score one point for each correct answer.

Face Test Response *(See pp. 26 and 27)*

Fit the names to the faces:

8 _____   7 _____

6 _____

1 _____   5 _____

3 _____   2 _____

9 _____

4 _____   10 _____

Score one point for each correct answer.

Date Test Response (*See p. 25*)

9 _____ French Revolution
6 _____ Battle of Waterloo
1 _____ Great Fire of London
10 _____ American Declaration of Independence
2 _____ Beethoven's birthday
5 _____ First printing press
4 _____ Russian Revolution
3 _____ Signing of Magna Carta
8 _____ Einstein's Theory of Relativity
7 _____ Invention of the telescope

Scoring: give yourself one point for an accurate answer and half a point if you come within five years. Ten points is a perfect score.

Now, below, calculate your total score for all the tests – perfect is 192.

Test Result Summary

Test	Your Score	Possible Total
Link Test		40
Peg Test		10
Number Test		60
Telephone Number Test		10
Card Test		52
Face Test		10
Dates Test		10
Total		192

To calculate Summary Per Cent Score:
Divide Your Score (YS) into the Possible Total $\left(\dfrac{PT}{YS} = x\right)$

Then divide the result (x) into 100 $\left(\dfrac{100}{x}\right)$

= Your Summary Per Cent Score

This completes your initial testing (there will be other tests for you to experiment with throughout the text). Normal scores on each of these tests range from 20 to 60 per cent. Even a score of 60 per cent, which in the average group will be considered excellent, is well below what you can expect of yourself when you have absorbed the information in this book. The average trained memoriser would have scored between 95 and 100 per cent on every one of the foregoing tests.

Onword

The next chapter outlines the history of memory, giving you a context in which to learn the memory techniques and systems, and shows how recently it is that we have begun to understand your amazing innate abilities.

The History
of Memory

3

From the time when man first began to depend on his mind for coping with his environment, the possession of an excellent memory has been a step to positions of command and respect. Throughout human history there have been recorded remarkable – sometimes legendary – feats of memory.

The Greeks

It is difficult to say exactly when and where the first integrated ideas on memory arose. The first sophisticated concepts, however, can be attributed to the Greeks, some 600 years before the birth of Christ. As we look back on them now, these 'sophisticated' ideas were surprisingly naïve, especially since some of the men proposing them are numbered among the greatest thinkers the world has ever known.

In the **sixth century BC**, Parmenides thought of memory as being a mixture of light and dark or heat and cold. He believed that as long as any given mixture remained unstirred, the memory would be perfect. As soon as the mixture was altered, forgetting occurred. Diogenes of Apollonia advanced a different theory, in the **fifth century** BC. He suggested that memory was a process that consisted of events producing an equal distribution of air in the body. Like Parmenides, he thought that when this equilibrium was disturbed, forgetting would occur.

Not surprisingly, the first person to introduce a really major idea in the field of memory was Plato, in the **fourth century** BC. His theory is known as the Wax Tablet Hypothesis and was still accepted until recently. To Plato, the mind accepted impressions in the same way that wax becomes marked when a pointed object is applied to its surface. Plato assumed that once the impression had been made it remained until it wore away with time, leaving a smooth surface once again. This smooth surface was, of course, what Plato considered to be equivalent to complete forgetting – the opposite aspect of the same process. As will become clear later, many people now feel that memory and forgetting are two quite different processes. Shortly after Plato, Zeno the Stoic slightly modified Plato's ideas, suggesting that sensations actually 'wrote' impressions on the wax tablet. Like those before him, when Zeno referred to the mind and its memory, he did not place it in any particular organ or section of the body. To him, as to all the Greeks, 'mind' was a very unclear concept.

The first man to introduce a more scientific terminology was Aristotle, in the **late fourth century** BC. He maintained that the language previously used was not adequate to explain the physical aspects of memory. In applying his new language Aristotle attributed to the heart most of the functions that we now attribute to the brain. Part of the heart's function, he realised, was concerned with the blood, and he felt that memory was based on the blood's movements. He thought that forgetting was the result of a gradual slowing down of these movements. Aristotle made another important contribution to the subject of memory when he introduced his laws of association of ideas. The concept of association of ideas and images is now known to be of major importance to memory. Throughout this book this concept will be discussed and applied.

In the **third century** BC, Herophilus introduced 'vital' and 'animal' spirits to the discussion. He thought that the vital, or 'higher order', spirits produced the 'lower order' animal spirits, which included the memory, the brain and the nervous system. All of these he thought to be secondary in importance to the heart. It is interesting to note that one reason advanced by Herophilus for man's superiority over animals was the large number of creases in his brain. (These creases are now known as the convolutions of the cortex.) Herophilus, however, offered no reason for his conclusion. It was not until the nineteenth century, more than 2000 years later, that the real importance of the cortex was discovered.

The Greeks, then, were the first to seek a physical as opposed to a spiritual basis for memory; they developed scientific concepts and a language structure that helped the development of these concepts; and they contributed the Wax Tablet Hypothesis, which suggested that memory and forgetting were opposite aspects of the same process.

The Romans

The theoretical contributions by the Romans to our knowledge of memory were surprisingly minimal. The major thinkers of their time, including Cicero in the **first century** BC and Quintilian in the **first century** AD, accepted without question the Wax Tablet Hypothesis of memory and did little further work on the subject. Their major and extremely important contributions were in the development of memory systems. They were the first to introduce the idea of a Link System and a Room System, both of which will be described in later chapters.

The Influence of the Christian Church

The next major contributor to memory theory was the great physician Galen in the **second century** AD. He located and delineated various anatomical and physiological structures and made further investigations into the function and structure of the nervous system. Like the later Greeks, he assumed that memory and mental processes were part of the lower order of animal spirits. He thought that these spirits were manufactured in the sides of the brain and that, consequently, memory was seated there. Galen thought that air was sucked into the brain and mixed with the vital spirits. This mixture produced animal spirits that were pushed down through the nervous system, enabling humans to experience sensation.

Galen's ideas on memory were rapidly accepted and condoned by the Church, which at this time was beginning to exert a great influence. His ideas became doctrine, and as a result little progress was made in the field for 1500 years. These intellectual strictures stifled some of the greatest minds that philosophy and science have produced. In the **fourth century** AD St Augustine accepted the

Church's idea that memory was a function of the soul and that the soul was located in the brain. He never expanded on the anatomical aspects of these ideas.

From the time of St Augustine until the **seventeenth century** there were almost no significant developments, and even in the seventeenth century new ideas were restricted by doctrine. Even so great a thinker as Descartes accepted Galen's basic ideas, although he thought that animal spirits were sent from the pineal gland on special courses through the brain until they came to the part where memory could be triggered. The more clear-cut these courses, the more readily, he thought, would they open when animal spirits travelled through them. It was in this way that he explained the improvement of memory and the development of what are known as memory traces. A memory trace is a physical change in the nervous system that was not present before learning. The trace enables us to recall.

Another great philosopher, who went along with the tide, was Thomas Hobbes, who discussed and considered the idea of memory but contributed little to what had already been said. He agreed with Aristotle's ideas, rejecting nonphysical explanations of memory. He did not, however, specify the real nature of memory, nor did he make any significant attempts to locate it accurately.

It is evident from the theories of the seventeenth-century intellectuals that the inhibiting influence of Galen and the Church had been profound. Practically all these great thinkers accepted without question primitive ideas on memory.

Transitional Period – the Eighteenth Century

One of the first thinkers to be influenced by the Renaissance and by the ideas of Newton was David Hartley in the **eighteenth century**, who developed the vibratory theory of memory. Applying Newton's ideas on vibrating particles, Hartley suggested that there were memory vibrations in the brain that began before birth. New sensations modified existing vibrations in degree, kind, place and direction. After being influenced by a new sensation, vibrations quickly returned to their natural state. But if the same sensation appeared again, the vibrations took a little longer to return. This progression would finally result in the vibrations remaining in their 'new' state, and a memory trace was thus established.

Other major thinkers of this period included Zanotti, who was the first to link electrical forces with brain functions, and Bonnet, who developed the ideas of Hartley in relation to the flexibility of nerve fibres. He felt that the more often nerves were used, the more easily they vibrated, and the better memory would be. The theories of these men were more sophisticated than previous ones because they had been largely influenced by developments in related scientific fields. This interaction of ideas laid the groundwork for some of the modern theories of memory.

The Nineteenth Century

With the development of science in Germany in the **nineteenth century**, some important advances occurred. Many of the ideas initiated by the Greeks were overthrown, and work on memory expanded to include the biological sciences.

Georg Prochaska, a Czech physiologist, finally and irrevocably rejected the age-old idea of animal spirits on the grounds that it had no scientific basis and that there was no evidence to support it. He felt that limited existing knowledge made speculation on the location of memory in the brain a waste of time. 'Spatial localisation may be possible,' he said, 'but we just do not know enough at the moment to make it a useful idea.' It was not for some 50 years that localising the area of memory function became a useful pursuit.

Another major theory presented in this century was that of Pierre Flourens, a French physiologist, who 'located' the memory in every part of the brain. He said that the brain acted as a whole and could not be considered as the interaction of elementary parts.

Modern Theories

Developments in memory research were aided to an enormous degree by advances in technology and methodology in the **twentieth century**. Almost without exception physiologists and other thinkers in this field agree that memory is located in the cerebrum, which is the large area of the brain covering the surface of the cortex. Even today, however, the exact localisation of memory areas is proving a difficult task, as is the accurate under-standing of the function of memory itself. Current thought has progressed from Hermann Ebbinghaus's work at the turn of the century, with regard to basic learning and forgetting curves (see chapter 11, page 79), to complex theories. Research and theory can be roughly divided into three main areas: work on establishing a biochemical basis for memory; theories suggesting that memory can no longer be considered as a single process but must be broken down into divisions; and the clinical surgeon Wilder Penfield's work on brain stimulation.

Research into the biochemical basis for memory was initiated in the **late 1950s**. This theory suggests that RNA (ribonucleic acid), a complex molecule, serves as a chemical mediator for memory. RNA is produced by the substance DNA (deoxyribonucleic acid), which is responsible for our genetic inheritance For example, DNA determines eye colour. A number of experiments have been performed with RNA that lend support to the idea that RNA does indeed have a lot to do with the way in which we remember things. In one instance, when animals were given certain types of training, the RNA found in specific cells was changed. And further, if the production of RNA in an animal's body was stopped or modified, this animal was unable to learn or remember. An even more exciting experiment showed that when RNA was taken from one rat and injected into another, the second rat 'remembered' things that he had never been taught but that the first rat had.

While research into this aspect of memory is progressing, other theorists are saying that we should stop emphasising 'memory' and concentrate more on the study of 'forgetting'. Their position is that we do not so much remember as gradually forget. Encompassing this idea is the duplex theory of remembering and forgetting, which states that there are two different kinds of information retention: long-term and short-term. For example, you have probably experienced a different 'feeling' in the way that you recall a telephone number that has just been given to you and the way that you recall your own telephone number. The short-term situation is one in which the idea is 'in' the brain but has not yet been properly coded and is therefore more readily forgotten. In the long-term situation the idea has been completely coded, filed and stored, and it will probably remain there for years, if not for life.

Research into direct brain stimulation was initiated by Dr Wilder Penfield. When performing craniotomies (removal of a small section of the brain) in order to reduce epileptic attacks, Penfield had first to remove a portion of the skull lying over the side of the brain. Before operating, Penfield conducted a systematic electrical stimulation of the open brain, and the patient, who remained conscious, reported his experience after each stimulation. In an early case Penfield stimulated the temporal lobe of the brain, and the patient reported a re-created memory of a childhood experience.

Penfield found that stimulating various areas of the cortex produces a range of responses but that only stimulation of the temporal lobes leads to reports of meaningful and integrated experiences. These experiences are often complete in that when re-created they include the colour, sound, movement and emotional content of the original experiences.

Of particular interest in these studies is the fact that some of the memories stimulated electrically by Penfield had been unavailable in normal recall. In addition, the stimulated experiences seemed to be far more specific and accurate than normal conscious recall, which tends to be a generalisation. It was Penfield's belief that the brain records every item to which it pays conscious attention and that this record is basically permanent, although it may be 'forgotten' in day-to-day living.

More recently, theorists have returned to a position similar to that of Flourens, in which they are suggesting that every part of the brain may include *all* memories. This model is based on holographic photography. In simple terms, a holographic photographic plate is simply a piece of glass, which, when two laser beams are passed through it at the right angle, reproduces a ghostly, three-dimensional photograph. One of the amazing things about this photographic plate is that if you smash it into 100 pieces and take any one of those 100 pieces, you can shine the two laser beams through it and still get the same (although slightly more blurred) picture. Thus every part of the holographic photographic plate contains a minirecord of the overall picture.

British scientist David Bohm and others are suggesting that the brain is similar. In other words, every one of our multimillion brain cells may, in fact, act as a minibrain, recording in some fantastically complex way, as yet indiscernible to our clumsy measuring instruments, our entire experience. Fantastic as this theory may sound, it goes a long way toward explaining the perfect memories we have in dreams, the surprise random recall, the memories of the perfect memorisers, the statistics from Rosensweig's experiments, the results of Penfield's experiments, the mathematical grandeur of Anokhin's results, and much of the near-death-type experiences.

As the twenty-first century (the Century of the Brain) dawns, we find ourselves on the threshold of a wondrous new world of knowledge about the brain and memory. This threshold is similar to that in astronomy when a few years ago the first major space probes and extraterrestrial telescopes were launched to explore the universe. Even as you read this book, around the world researchers and scientists are making astounding new discoveries about your amazing brain and the incredible potential of your memory.

How Many Brains?

Supplementing this modern research has been the new discovery that we have not one brain but many. Professor Roger Sperry recently received the Nobel Prize for his breakthrough work in this area. Sperry discovered that each one of us has a brain that is divided into two upper physiological sections, each dealing with different mental functions.

In the 1980s Sperry's work has been continued by Professor Eran Zaidel, who has shown that the range of cortical skills is much more widely distributed than had originally been thought. Zaidel has demonstrated that *both* cerebral hemispheres seem to have a latent ability to perform the full range of cortical skills.

These skills, which we now know are attributable to the *entire* cortex, were originally thought to be divided into the left and right hemispheres in the following way:

The left side of the cortex processes in the following manner:

1   logic
2   words
3   lists
4   number
5   sequence
6   linearity
7   analysis

Similarly, in most of us, the right side of the cortex processes with the following mental functions:

1   rhythm
2   imagination
3   daydreaming
4   colour
5   dimension
6   spatial awareness
7   *Gestalt* (whole picture)

This is your superstreamlined brain, depicted as if viewed with X-ray eyes from a vantage point to the left of the left shoulder. Thus, you are looking at the left cortex, which deals with the mental functions of logic, words, lists, number, sequence, linearity and analysis. The right side of the cortex, the back tip of which you can just see, deals with rhythm, imagination, daydreaming, colour, dimension, spatial awareness and *Gestalt*. These two ranges of abilities *combine* to give you a super-powered memory.

Sperry and others also found that the more people use both sides of their brains together, the more the use of each side benefits the other. For example, it was found that the study of music helped the study of mathematics, and the study of mathematics helped the study of music; that the study of rhythm helped the study of languages and that the study of languages helped the learning of bodily rhythms; that the study of dimension helped the study of mathematics and that the study of mathematics helped the brain conceptualise dimension; and so on. It was similarly found that if a person used more of these areas, the more generally capable was his entire memory *and* the more enjoyable was the entire process.

Onword

No matter what you have been taught, somewhere latent within each of you lies each one of these capabilities simply waiting to be freed.

The Secret Principles Underlying a Superpower Memory

4

Preview
- The Memory Principles
- Key Memory Image Words

The Greeks so worshipped memory that they made a goddess out of her – Mnemosyne. It was her name from which was derived the current word *mnemonics*, used to describe memory techniques such as those you are about to learn.

In Greek and Roman times senators would learn mnemonic techniques in order to impress other politicians and the public with their phenomenal powers of learning and memory. Using these simple but sophisticated methods the Romans were able to remember, without fault, thousands of items, including statistics relating to their empire, and became the rulers of their time.

Long before we had discovered the physiological breakdown of the functions in the left and right cortical structures the Greeks had intuitively realised that there are two underlying principles that ensure perfect memory:

imagination
association

Whereas, in current times, most of us are actively discouraged from using our imaginative abilities, and consequently learn very little about the nature of mental association, the Greeks emphasised these two foundation stones of mental functioning and opened the way for us to develop the techniques even further.

Quite simply if you want to remember *anything*, all you have to do is to *associate* (link) it with *some known or fixed item* (the memory systems in this book will give you those easily remembered fixed items), calling upon your *imagination* throughout.

The Memory Principles

The principles for perfect memory laid down by the Greeks fit in *exactly* with the information recently discovered about the left and right cortex. Without a scientific basis, the Greeks realised that in order to remember well, you have to use every aspect of your mind. These principles will be outlined in this chapter.

In order to remember well, you must include in your associated and linked mental landscape the following twelve Memory Principles, which can be remembered with the mnemonic of the initial letters, SMASHIN' SCOPE:

1 ● Synaesthesia/Sensuality

Synaesthesia refers to the blending of the senses. Most of the great 'natural' memorisers and all of the great mnemonists developed an increased sensitivity in each of their senses, and then blended these senses to produce enhanced recall. In developing the memory it was found to be essential to sensitise increasingly and train regularly your senses of:

a) vision   e) touch
b) hearing   f) kinaesthesia – your
c) smell   awareness of bodily position
d) taste   and movement in space.

2 ● Movement

In any mnemonic image, movement adds another giant range of possibilities for your brain to 'link in' and thus remember. As your images move, make them three-dimensional. As a subdivision of movement, use rhythm in your memory images. The more rhythm and variation of rhythm in your mental picture, the more they will be outstanding and thus the more they will be remembered.

3 ● Association

Whatever you wish to memorise, make sure you associate or link it to something stable in your mental environment, i.e. Peg System:

one = paintbrush (see page 54). See also The Link System (*chapter 5, page 49*).

4 ● Sexuality

We all have a good memory in this area. Use it!

5 ● Humour

The more funny, ridiculous, absurd and surreal you make your images, the more outstandingly memorable they will be. Have fun with your memory.

6 ● Imagination

This is the powerhouse of your memory. Einstein said, 'Imagination is more important than knowledge. For knowledge is limited, whereas imagination embraces the entire world, stimulating progress, giving birth to evolution.' The more you apply your vivid imagination to memory, the better your memory will be. (Memory Foundation)

7 ● Number

Numbering adds specificity and efficiency to the principle of order and sequence.

8 ● Symbolism

Substituting a more meaningful image for a normal, boring or abstract concept increases the probability of recall, or using traditional symbols, e.g. stop sign or light bulb.

9 ● Colour

Whenever possible, use the full range of the rainbow (ideally vibrant/highlighter), to make your ideas more 'colourful' and therefore more memorable.

10 ● Order and/or Sequence

In combination with the other principles, order and/or sequence allows for much more immediate reference, and increases the brain's possibilities for 'random access'. Examples are: little to big, colour grouping, sorting by category, and hierarchical aggregation.

11 ● Positive Images

In most instances positive and pleasant images were found to be better for memory purposes, because they made the brain want to return to the images. Certain negative images, even though applying all the principles above, and though in and of themselves 'memorable' could be blocked by the brain because it found the prospect of returning to such images unpleasant.

12 ● Exaggeration

In all your images, exaggerate size (large and small), shape and sound and therefore memorability.

Brain Bites

The basic Memory Principles can themselves be memorised by using an acronym. They have been ordered on the preceding pages to make the phrase SMASHIN' SCOPE, which confirms the 'smashin' scope' of your limitless memory.

Key Memory Image Words

In each memory system there is a Key Word. This word is the 'Key Memory Word' in that it is the constant peg on which you will hang other items you wish to remember. This Key Memory Word is specifically designed to be an 'Image Word' in that it *must* produce a picture or image in the mind of the person using the memory system. Thus the phrase 'Key Memory Image Word'.

Purity

As you progress through the increasingly sophisticated mnemonic systems outlined in the following chapters, you will realise the importance of being sure that the pictures you build in your mind contain only the items you want to remember, and those items/words must be associated with or connected to Key Memory Images. The connections between your basic Memory System Images and the things you wish to remember should be as fundamental, pure and uncomplicated as possible.

This may be accomplished as follows:

1 Crashing things together
2 Sticking things together
3 Placing things on top of each other
4 Placing things underneath each other
5 Placing things inside each other

6   Substituting things for each other
7   Placing things in new situations
8   Weaving things together
9   Wrapping things together
10   Having things talk
11   Having things dance
12   Having things share their colour, aroma, action

By now it will be clear to you that the systems worked out by the Greeks, and for nearly 2000 years discarded as mere tricks, were in fact based on the way in which the human brain actually functions. The ancients realised the importance of words, order, sequence and number, now known to be functions of the left side of the cortex; and imagination, colour, rhythm, dimension and daydreaming, now known to be right-cortex functions.

Mnemosyne was to the Greeks the most beautiful of all the goddesses, proved by the fact that Zeus spent more time in her bed than in that of any other goddess or mortal. He slept with her for nine days and nights, and the result of that coupling was the birth of the nine Muses, the goddesses who preside over love poetry, epic poetry, hymns, dance, comedy, tragedy, music, history and astronomy. For the Greeks, then, the infusion of energy (Zeus) into memory (Mnemosyne) produced both creativity and knowledge.

They were correct. If you apply the Mnemonic Principles and Techniques appropriately, not only will your memory improve in the areas outlined in this book but your creativity will soar, and with these twin improvements your overall mental functioning and assimilation of knowledge will accelerate at the same fantastic pace. You will be developing a new and dynamic synthesis between the left and right cortex of your brain.

Onword

The following chapters take you from the very simple systems through to the more advanced systems, concluding with Mind Maps, the Star of the Memorisers' Solar System, which will enable you to remember *thousands* of items. So that you can maintain the extraordinary results that you are going to achieve, a final chapter shows you how to maintain your memory over a long period of future time.

The Link System 5

- Link System Memory Test

In this chapter you will see for yourself that your memory can improve, and that by improving it, your imaginative powers and your creativity will also be released.

The Link System is the most basic of all the memory systems and will give you a foundation with which to make learning the most advanced systems extremely easy. This basic system is used for memorising short lists of items, such as shopping lists, in which each item is linked to or associated with the next. While using this system, you will be using all of these twelve Memory Principles:

Synaesthesia/Sensuality
Movement
Association
Sexuality
Humour
Imagination
Number
Symbolism
Colour
Order and/or sequence
Positive images
Exaggeration

You will also be using the six senses of:

> Taste
> Touch
> Smell
> Sight
> Hearing
> Rhythm/kinaesthesia

In using all these Principles and skills you will be exercising the dynamic relationship between your left and right cortex and your senses, thereby increasing the overall power of your brain. Imagine, for example, that you have been asked to shop for the following items:

> a silver serving spoon
> six drinking glasses
> bananas
> pure soap
> eggs
> biological washing powder
> dental floss
> wholewheat bread
> tomatoes
> roses

Instead of scrambling around for little bits of paper (everyone has either done it himself or seen others desperately fumbling through their pockets for the missing slip) or trying to remember all the items by simple repetition and consequently forgetting at least two or three, you would simply apply the Memory Principles as follows:

Imagine yourself walking out of your front door perfecting the most amazing balancing trick: in your mouth is the most enormous silver-coloured serving spoon, the handle-end of which you are holding between your teeth, as you *taste* and *feel* the metal in your mouth.

Carefully balanced in the ladle-end of the spoon are six *exaggeratedly* beautiful crystal glasses, through which the sunlight reflects brilliantly into your bedazzled eyes. As you look with delighted amazement at the glasses, you can also *hear* them deliberately tinkling on the silver spoon. Going outside into the street, you step on the most *gigantic yellow and brown coloured* banana, which *skids* with a *swish* from under you. Being a fantastic balancer, you barely manage not to fall and confidently place your other foot groundward only to find that you have stepped on a shimmering white bar of pure soap. This being too much for even a master, you fall backward and land seat down on a mound of eggs. As you sink into them, you can *hear* the cracking of the shells, *see* the yellow of the yolk and the white of the albumen, and *feel* the dampness soaking into your clothes. (See Colour Plate I, opposite page 96.)

Using your *imaginative* ability to *exaggerate* anything, you speed up time and *imagine* that, in a couple of seconds, you have gone back inside, undressed, washed your soiled clothes in a super biological washing powder, called pure soap, which allows pure, shimmering water to leave the washing machine, and then visualise yourself once again on your way out of the front door. This time, because you are slightly tired by the previous accident, you are pulling yourself along towards the shops on a *gigantic* rope made of *millions* of threads of dental floss, the rope *connecting* your front door to the chemist's shop.

Just as all this exertion begins to make you feel hungry, wafting on the warm wind comes an *incredibly strong aroma* of freshly baked wholewheat bread. *Imagine* yourself being dragged by the nose as you salivate *extraordinarily* thinking of the *taste* of the freshly baked bread. As you enter the baker's shop, you notice to your amazement that every loaf on the baker's shelves is filled with *brilliantly pulsating red* tomatoes, the baker's latest idea for a new food fad.

As you walk out of the baker's shop, *noisily* munching on your tomato and wholewheat loaf, you see walking down the road with the most amazing *rhythm* the *sexiest* person you have ever seen (really let your imagination go on this one). Your immediate instinct is to buy the person roses, so you dive into the nearest flower shop, which sells nothing but red roses, and buy the lot, *bedazzled* by the *greenness* of the leaves, the *redness* of the flowers, the *feel* of the flowers as you carry them, the *feel* of the thorns, and the *fragrance* from the roses themselves.

When you have finished reading this fantasy, close your eyes and run back through the image-story you have just completed. If you think you can already remember all ten items in the shopping list, turn now to the next page and fill in the answers. If not, read through this chapter again, carefully visualising on your mind's inner screen, in sequence, the events of the story. Turn to the next page when you are ready.

Memory Test

Note here the ten items you had to buy.

[handwritten list]
- clipper
- eggs
- fire soap
- dental floss
- bread
- silver spoon
- bananas

If you scored 7 or more, you are already in the top 1 per cent of scores for the memorisation of such a list. And you have now used the basic keys for unlocking much of the limitless potential of your brain.

Onword

Practise the Link System on a couple of lists of your own devising, making sure that you use the Memory Principles throughout, remembering that the more imaginative, absurd and sensual you can be, the better. When you have had a little practice with the Link System, move on to the next chapter.

The Number-Shape System 6

In chapter 5 you learned the Link System, in which you applied all the Memory Principles with the exception of number and order. We now move on to the first of the Peg Memory Systems.

A Peg Memory System differs from the Link System in that it uses a special list of Key Memory Images that never change and to which everything that you wish to remember can be linked and associated. A Peg System can be thought of much like a wardrobe containing a certain definite number of hangers on which you hang your clothes. The hangers themselves never change, but the clothes that are hung on them vary infinitely. In the Number-Shape System, which is the first of the Peg Systems covered, the number and shape represent the hangers, and the things you wish to remember with the system represent the clothes to be hung on the hangers. The system is an easy one and uses only the numbers from 1 to 10.

The best system is one you will create yourself – rather than one supplied for you. This is because minds are infinitely varied, and the associations, links and images that you may have will generally be different from mine and everyone else's. The associations and images you generate from your own creative imagination will last far longer and be much more effective than any that could be 'implanted'. I shall therefore explain exactly how you can construct a system and shall then give examples of its practical use.

In the Number-Shape System, all you have to do is think of images for each of the numbers from 1 to 10, each image reminding you of the number because both the image and the number have the same shape. For example, and to make your task a little easier, the Key Number-Shape Memory Word that most people use for the number 2 is *swan* because the number 2 is shaped like a swan, and similarly because a swan looks like a living, elegant version of the number 2.

In the Number-Shape System, images that 'look like' the number are used as hangers, or hooks, on which to link items you wish to remember. For example, a common Key Image for the number 2 is a swan.

Listed opposite are the numbers from 1 to 10, with a blank beside each number for you to pencil in the various words that you think *best* image the shape of the numbers. As you select the words, try to make sure that they are exceptionally good *visual* images, with lots of good colour and basic imagination-potential within them. They should be images to which you will be able to link the things you wish to remember with ease and enjoyment, using the *SMASHIN' SCOPE* of your memory.

Here are several examples:

1 **Paintbrush,** pole, pencil, pen, penis, straw, candle
2 **Swan**, duck, goose
3 **Heart**, breasts, double chin, behind, molehills
4 **Yacht**, table, chair
5 **Hook**, cymbal and drum, pregnant woman
6 **Elephant's trunk**, golf club, cherry, pipe
7 **Cliff**, fishing line, boomerang
8 **Snowman**, bun, hourglass, shapely woman
9 **Balloon and stick**, tennis racquet, sperm, tadpole, flag
10 **Bat and ball**, Laurel and Hardy

Give yourself not more than ten minutes to complete the list from 1 to 10, and even if you find some numbers difficult, don't worry; just read on.

Number	Select Your Own Number-Shape Memory Words
1	*Pencil*
2	*Swan*
3	*Bum*
4	*4*
5	
6	
7	
8	
9	
10	

Now that you have generated several of your own number-images and have seen other suggestions, you should select the Number-Shape Key Memory *Image* for each number that is the best one for you.

When you have done this, draw in overleaf your appropriate image for each number. (Don't feel inhibited if you consider yourself not good at art; your right brain needs the practice.) The more colours you can use in your images, the better.

At the end of this paragraph you should close your eyes and test yourself by mentally running through the numbers from 1 to 10 in order. As you come to each number, mentally link it with the Number-Shape Key Memory Image you have selected and drawn, using the Memory Principles throughout, especially exaggeration, colour and movement. Make sure you actually *see* the images on the videoscreen of your closed eyelids, or hear, experience, taste or smell them. When you have done this exercise once, run through the numbers in reverse order, again linking them with your chosen word and again applying the Memory Principles. Next, pick out numbers randomly and as quickly as you can, making a game to see how quickly the image comes to mind. And finally reverse the whole process by flashing the images on your internal videoscreen, seeing how quickly you can connect the basic numbers to your images. Do this exercise now.

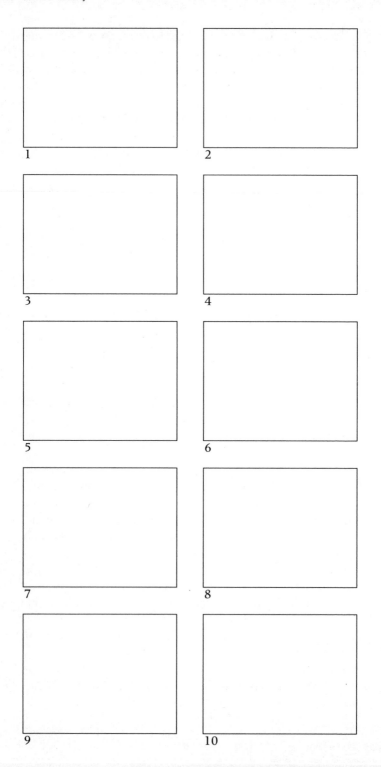

1

2

3

4

5

6

7

8

9

10

You have already accomplished a memory feat most people would find difficult. You have forged into your memory and creative imagination a system you will be able to use throughout your life and that combines the qualities of both the left and right of your brain.

The use of the system is simple and enjoyable and involves the major memory devices: **linking/association/imagination**. For example, if you have a list of ten items you wish to remember not simply by linking, as in the previous chapter, but in numerical order, reverse numerical order and random numerical order, the Number-Shape System makes the whole process easy.

Assume you wish to remember the following list of items:

1	Symphony	6	Sunshine
2	Prayer	7	Apple pie
3	Watermelon	8	Blossoms
4	Volcano	9	Spaceship
5	Motorcycle	10	Field of wheat

To remember these items in any order, all that you have to do is to link them with the appropriate Number-Shape Key Memory Image. As with the Link System, and all memory systems, the Memory Principles should be applied throughout; the more imaginative you can be, the better. Allow not more than three minutes to complete your memorisation of these ten items, using the Number-Shape System, then fill in the answers below. Fill in both your Number-Shape Image Words and the items you were asked to remember with each number. If you feel confident, start now; if not, you may find it helpful first to read the examples on pages 58–9.

	Peg Word		**Item**
1	Symphony Pencil	Symphony
2	Swan	Prayer
3	Bun	Watermelon
4	Yacht	Volcano
5	Hook	Motorcycle
6	Trunk	Sunlight
7	Cliff	Apple Pie
8	Ball	Blossom
9	Pennant	Space ship
10	Batt Ball	Wheat field

As a guide for those who might have had a little difficulty with this exercise, the following are examples of possible ways in which the ten items to be memorised might have been linked to the Number-Shape Key Memory Images:

1 For **symphony** you might have imagined a conductor conducting frantically with a gigantic **paintbrush**, splattering paint over most of the musicians; or you might have imagined all the violinists playing their instruments with straws; or again you might have imagined them all with gigantic penises. Whatever your image, the Memory Principles should be applied.

2 **Prayer** is an abstract word. It is often mistakenly assumed that abstract words are hard to memorise. Using proper memory techniques, you will find that this is not the case, as you may have already discovered. All you have to do is to 'image' the abstract in concrete form. You might have to imagine your **swan** or duck or goose with its wings upheld like hands in prayer; or fill an imaginary church with imaginary swans, geese or ducks being led in a prayer service by a minister who was also a bird.

3 Easy!

4 You might have imagined your gigantic **volcano** within the ocean, seeing it erupting red and furiously beneath your **yacht**, the steam and hissing created by the volcano actually heaving your yacht right off the water; or you might have had your volcano miniaturised and placed on a chair on which you were about to sit (you would certainly *feel* it); or imagined a mountainous table actually blocking the power of the volcano.

5 A giant **hook** might have come down from the sky and lifted you and your **motorcycle** off the road along which you were speeding; or you on your motorcycle might have driven, incredibly noisily and disruptively, into a musical instrument shop, knocking over cymbals and drums; or seated astride the motorcycle is an enormous pregnant woman.

6 **Sunshine** could be pouring out of an **elephant's trunk**; or you might have flung the golf club rhythmically up into the air, and it got entangled in a sunbeam and drawn

toward the sun; or the sunbeam could be zapping like a laser into a cherry, making it grow gigantic before your very eyes, and you imagine the taste as you bite into it, the juices dribbling down your chin.

7   Your gigantic **cliff** could actually be made entirely of **apple pie**; or your fishing line could catch, instead of a fish, a bedraggled, soggy but nevertheless still scrumptious apple pie; or your boomerang could fly off into the distance and, with a thunk, end up in an apple pie as big as a mountain, not returning to you but sending only the delicious smells of the apple and the piecrust.

8   Your **snowman** could be decorated entirely with exquisitely pink **blossoms**; or your hourglass could tell the time not by the falling of sand but by the gentle falling of millions of tiny blossoms within the hourglass; or your shapely woman could be walking provocatively through endless fields of waist-high fallen blossoms.

9   You could miniaturise your **spaceship** and make it into a **balloon and stick**; or miniaturise it even further and have it as the leading sperm about to fertilise an egg; or imagine it leaving Earth's atmosphere with a huge flag on its nose.

10   You feel the shock in your **bat** as it cracks against the **ball**, and you see the ball sailing across endless **fields** of rhythmically waving, beautifully golden **wheat**; or you image Laurel and Hardy playing the ultimate fools and thrashing around, while tramping, the same endless fields of wheat.

These are, of course, only examples, and are included to indicate the kind of exaggeration, imagination, sensuality and creative thinking that is necessary to establish the most effective memory links. As with the Link System, it is essential that you practise this system on your own. I recommend giving yourself at least one test before you move to the next chapter.

One of the best ways to do this is to check yourself with members of your family or with friends. Ask them to make up a list of any ten items and to read the list to you with about a five- to ten-second pause between each item. The instant they have given you the item to be memorised, make the most wild, colourful, exaggerated associations possible, projecting images onto your internal screen, and thus consolidating them as you progress. You (and they) will be amazed at the ease with which you can remember the items, and it is most impressive when you are able to repeat them in reverse and random order.

Don't worry about confusing previous lists of items with new ones. As mentioned at the beginning of the chapter, this particular Peg System can be compared to coat hangers – you simply remove one coat (association) and replace it with another.

In the next chapter I shall introduce a second system based on the numbers 1 to 10: the Number-Rhyme System. These two systems can then be combined to enable you to remember twenty items with as much facility as you have just remembered ten. In subsequent chapters more sophisticated systems will be introduced to allow you to store lists of items stretching into the thousands. These systems are recommended for long-term memory, the things you wish to retain over a long period of time. The Number-Shape System you have just learned and the Number-Rhyme System you are about to learn are recommended for your short-term memory purposes – those items you wish to remember for only a few hours.

Onword

Give yourself about a day to become skilled in using the techniques you have learned so far before moving to the next chapter.

The Number-Rhyme System

- Number-Shape and Number-Rhyme Memory Test

You will find the Number-Rhyme System especially easy to learn, since it is identical in principle to the Number-Shape System. Also, like the Number-Shape System, it can be used for remembering short lists of items that you need to store in your memory for only a brief time.

In the Number-Rhyme system, as before, you use the numbers from 1 to 10, and instead of having Key Memory Images that resemble the shape of the number, you devise Key Memory Images represented by a word that *rhymes* with the sound of the number. For example, the Key Rhyming Memory Image Word that most people use for the number 5 is *hive*, the images that they use ranging from one enormous hive from which emanates a sky-covering swarm of monster bees to a microscopic hive with only one tiny bee.

As with the Link System and the Number-Shape System, it is essential to apply the Memory Principles, making each image as imaginative, colourful and sensual as you possibly can. As in the previous chapter, you will find listed the numbers from 1 to 10, with a blank beside each for you to pencil in the Rhyming Image Word that you think will produce the best image for each number. Make sure that the images will be good memory hooks for you. You may select them from the list on page 62.

By now your associative and creative thinking abilities will have improved your mental capacity, so give yourself not ten minutes as before but six minutes to fill in your initial Key Image Words.

Number	Select Your Own Number-Rhyme Image Word
1	*Bun*
2	*Door*
3	*Tree*
4	*Door*
5	*Hive*
6	*BRICKS*
7	*HEAVEN*
8	*SKATE*
9	*WINE*
10	*MEN*

As before, I am going to offer a few alternative image ideas commonly used. Consider these and your own Key Rhyming Image Words, and select for each number, from 1 to 10, the one you consider to be best for you:

1 **Bun**, sun, nun, Hun, run, fun
2 **Shoe**, pew, loo, crew, gnu, coo, moo
3 **Tree**, flea, sea, knee, see, free
4 **Door**, moor, boar, paw, pour
5 **Hive**, drive, chive, dive, jive
6 **Sticks**, bricks, wicks, kicks, licks
7 **Heaven**, Devon, leaven
8 **Skate**, bait, gate, ate, date
9 **Vine**, wine, twine, line, dine, pine
10 **Hen**, pen, den, wren, men, yen

Having chosen the most appropriate Key Rhyming Image Word, draw your image, using as much imagination and colour as possible, in the space provided opposite.

After you have finished reading this paragraph, test yourself with your chosen Key Rhyming Image. Close your eyes, and run through the numbers 1 to 10, projecting onto your inner screen a clear and brilliant picture of the Key Rhyming Image you have for each number. First, run through the system from 1 to 10 in the normal order; next, run through the system in reverse order; next, run through the system in random order; finally, pick the images 'out of the air', and connect the numbers to them. As you do each exercise, repeat it, making each repetition faster than the previous

1

2

3

4

5

6

7

8

9

10

one, until you acquire such skill that your mind will instantaneously produce the image as soon as you think of the number. Spend at least five minutes on this exercise, starting now.

Now that you have mastered the Number-Rhyme System, you will see that it can be used in exactly the same way as the Number-Shape System.

Having learned both these systems, you have not only two separate 1 to 10 systems but also the makings of a system that allows you to remember *twenty* objects in standard sequence, reverse sequence and random sequence. All you have to do is to establish one of these two systems as the numbers from 1 to 10, letting the other system represent the numbers from 11 to 20. Decide which system you want to be which, and immediately put it to the test!

Give yourself approximately five minutes to memorise the list given below. When your time is up, fill in the answers as explained in the paragraph below.

1	Atom	11	Glitter
2	Tree	12	Heater
3	Stethoscope	13	Railway
4	Sofa	14	Lighter
5	Alley	15	Wart
6	Tile	16	Star
7	Windscreen	17	Peace
8	Honey	18	Button
9	Brush	19	Pram
10	Toothpaste	20	Pump

Number-Shape and Number-Rhyme Memory Test

Opposite are three columns of 20 numbers: the first in standard order; the second in reverse order; the third in random order. Complete each list, filling in, next to the number, the appropriate item from the list you have just memorised, covering the lists with your hand or with paper as you complete them and start on the next. When you have finished, calculate your score out of a possible 60 points.

1	ATOM	20	PUMP	11	
2		19	PRAM	15	WART
3	STGATHASORG	18	BATON	10	TOOTHPAST
4	SOFA	17	PEACE	3	STGATHASCORG
5		16	STAR	17	PEACE
6	TILE	15	WART	20	PUMP
7	WINDSCREEN	14	LIGHTER	4	SOFA
8	HONEY	13		9	BRUSH
9	BRUSH	12	STGATHA RADA 5		
10	TOOTHPASTE	11		19	PRAM
11		10	TOOTHPASTE	8	HONEY
12		9	BRUSH	13	
13		8	HONEY	1	ATOM
14	LIGHTER	7	WINDSCREEN	18	BATON
15	WART	6	TILE	7	WINDSCREEN
16	STAR	5		16	STAR
17	PEARL	4	SOFA	6	TILE
18	BATON	3	STGATHASCOR	12	RADIATOR
19	PRAM	2		2	
20	PUMP	1	ATOM	14	LIGHTER

Score, out of 60 points: 47

If it initially doesn't work perfectly . . .

You will almost certainly have made an improvement over your performance in the original test, but you might find that you are still having difficulty with certain associations. Check any such 'weak' associations and examine the reasons for any failure. These reasons usually include: associations that you don't like; too close or too similar associations; not enough exaggeration and imagination; not enough colour; not enough movement; weak links; not enough sensuality; and not enough humour. Take confidence from the fact that the more you practise, the more such weak links will become a matter of history. Today and tomorrow test yourself whenever possible. Ask as many of your friends and acquaintances as possible to challenge you on lists that they make up for you to remember.

On the first few attempts, you will undoubtedly make some errors, but even so you will be performing far beyond the average. Consider any errors and mistakes you make to be good opportunities for examining – and subsequently strengthening – any areas of weakness in your memory systems and the way you apply them. If you persevere, you will soon be able to fire back lists given to you without any hesitation and without any fear of failure. You will then be able to use the systems confidently – for pleasure, for entertainment, for practical use, and for exercising your general memory.

As you become more skilled, keep a continuing and growing list of the areas in your life in which you will apply the systems you are currently learning.

Onword

In the next chapter you will learn the basic system used and developed by the first recorded masters of mnemonics, the Romans.

The Roman Room System 8

The Romans were great inventors and practitioners of mnemonic
techniques, one of their most popular being the Roman Room.

The Romans constructed their memory system easily. They
imagined the entrance to their house and their room and then
filled the room with as many objects and items of furniture as they
chose – each object and piece of furniture serving as a link-image
onto which they attached the things they wished to remember.
The Romans were particularly careful not to make a mental
rubbish dump of their room; precision and order (attributes of the
left side of your cortex) are essential in this system.

A Roman might, for example, have constructed his imaginary
entrance and room with two gigantic pillars at either side of the
front door, a carved lion's head as his doorknob, and an exquisite
Greek statue on the immediate left as he walked in. Next to the
statue might have been a large sofa covered with the fur of one of
the animals the Roman had hunted; next to the sofa a flowering
plant; and, in front of the sofa, a large marble table on which were
placed goblets, a wine container, a bowl of fruit, and so forth.

Let's say that the Roman then wished to remember to buy a
pair of sandals, to get his sword sharpened, to buy a new servant,
to tend to his grapevine, to polish his helmet, to buy a present for
his child, and so on. He would simply imagine the first pillar at the
entrance of his imaginary room festooned with thousands of
sandals, the leather polished and glistening, and the smell
delighting his nostrils; he would imagine sharpening his sword on

the right-hand pillar, hearing the scraping as he did so, and feeling the blade as it became sharper and sharper; his servant he would imagine riding a roaring lion, while grapes he might remember by imagining his exquisite statue totally entwined with a grapevine on which were luscious grapes that he could imagine seeing and tasting so well that he would actually salivate; his helmet he could imagine by substituting the container of his imaginary flowering plant with the helmet itself; finally, he could imagine himself on his sofa, his arm around the child for whom he wished to buy a gift. (See Colour Plate II.)

The Roman Room System is particularly amenable to the application of the left and right cortical skills, and to the Memory Principles, because it requires very precise structuring and ordering, as well as a lot of imagination and sensuality. The delight of this system is that the room can be *entirely* imaginary, so you can have in it every wonderful item that you wish: things that please all your senses, items of furniture and objects of art you have always desired to possess in real life, and similarly foods and decorations that especially appeal to you. Another major advantage of using this system is that if you begin to imagine yourself in possession of certain items that exist in your imaginary room, both your memory and creative intelligence will begin to work paraconsciously on ways in which you can actually acquire such objects, increasing the probability that you will eventually do so.

The Roman Room System eliminates all boundaries on your imagination and allows you to remember as many items as you wish. On page 69 there is space for you to jot down quickly your first thoughts on the items you would like to have in your room, the shape and design of your room, and so on. When you have completed this, draw your ideal Memory Room on page 70, either as an artist's drawing or as an architect's plan, drawing, and printing in the names of, items with which you are going to furnish and decorate it.

First select ten specific loci for your memory items, building up to 20, 30, 50, etc., adding rooms to your house (or your castle, village, city, country, galaxy or universe!).

Many people find this to be their favourite memory system, and they use enormous sheets of paper on which they include hundreds of items in a gigantic room. If you wish to do this, by all means do so.

When you have completed this task, take a number of 'mental walks' around your room, memorising precisely the order, position and number of items in the room and similarly sensing with *all* your senses the colours, tastes, feels, smells and sounds within your room, using your whole range of cortical abilities.

Brain Bites

The first and six-time World Memory Champion, Dominic O'Brien, uses Roman Rooms, routes and memory maps in his memory competitions.

Onword

As with the previous memory systems you have learned, practise memorising using the Roman Room System both alone and with friends, until the system is a firmly established technique.

Roman Room: Initial Thoughts

_____

_____

_____

_____

_____

_____

_____

_____

_____

_____

Memory Room

The Alphabet System 9

The Alphabet System is the final Peg System and is similar in construction to the Number-Shape and Number-Rhyme Systems, the only difference being that, instead of using numbers, it uses the letters of the alphabet.

As with all the other memory systems, the Memory Principles apply to the Alphabet System. The rules for constructing your Alphabet Memory System are simple; they are as follows: you select a Key Memory Image Word that starts with the *sound* of the letter and is easily memorised. If you think of several possibilities for a letter, use the one that comes first in the dictionary. For example, for the letter *L* it would be possible to use *el*astic, *el*egy, *el*ephant, *el*bow, *el*m, etc. If you were looking up these words in the dictionary, the first one you would come to would be elastic, and that is therefore the word you would select for your Alphabet System. The reason for this rule is that if you should ever forget your Alphabet Key Image Word, you can mentally flick through the letters of the alphabet in order, rapidly arriving at the correct word. In the example given, if you had forgotten your Alphabet System image for the letter *L*, you would try *ela* and would immediately be able to recall your Key Image Word, *elastic*.

Another rule in the construction of your Alphabet System is that if the letter itself makes a word (for example *I* makes the word *eye*, and *J* makes the word *jay*, the bird), then that word should be used. In some cases, it is possible to use meaningful initials instead of complete words – for example, U.N.

Below are listed the letters of the alphabet. Paying close attention to the now-familiar rules for constructing a system, pencil in your own initial Alphabet System Image Words after looking at the list opposite.

Letter	Alphabet Image Word
A	
B	
C	
D	
E	
F	
G	
H	
I	
J	
K	
L	
M	
N	
O	
P	
Q	
R	
S	
T	
U	
V	
W	
X	
Y	
Z	

Now that you have completed your initial thoughts, recheck the Alphabet Image Words, making sure you have started your words with the *sound* of the letter or letter-word and not simply the letter itself. For example, *ant, bottle, case, dog* and *eddy* would not be correct Alphabet System Image Words because they do not start with the *sound* of the letter as it is pronounced when you are reciting the alphabet. Having rechecked your own words, now compare them with the list of suggestions opposite, and when you have done so, select your final list.

A   Ace
B   Bee (the letter makes a word; such a word should be used in all cases)
C   Sea (the same rule applies)
D   Deed (legal, though the initials DDT may be preferred)
E   Easel
F   Effervescence
G   Jeep (or jeans)
H   H-bomb
I   Eye
J   Jay
K   Cake
L   Elastic (or *elbow*, if you pronounce *elastic* with a long *e*)
M   MC (emcee)
N   Enamel (or entire, if you pronounce enamel with a long e)
O   Oboe
P   Pea
Q   Queue
R   Arch
S   Eskimo
T   Tea (or perhaps T-square)
U   Yew
V   Vehicle (or the initials V.P.)
W   WC
X   X-ray
Y   Wife
Z   Z-bend

Now make your final choices and draw your images below and on pages 74 to 76:

A

B

C

D

E

F

G

H

I

J

K

L

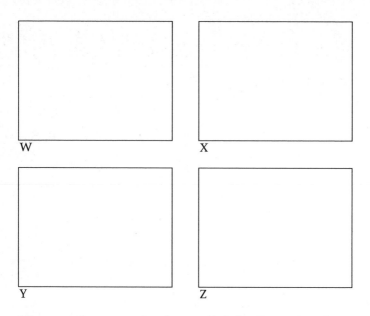

W	X
Y	Z

When you have completed your Alphabet Image-Word Images, review them in exactly the same way as with the previous memory systems, mentally visualising them in standard order, reverse order and random order. Similarly, make sure you test the system individually, and then with family or friends.

Onword

Now you have learned the introductory, basic Link and Peg Memory Systems. From now on, apart from a brief summary of these concepts in the next chapter, you will be learning more advanced, expansive and sophisticated systems that will enable you to remember dates, jokes, languages, information for examinations, names and faces, books, dreams, and lists of hundreds, even thousands, of items.

How to increase by 100 Per Cent

10

Everything You Have Learned So Far

You have now completed the five individual Memory Systems: Link, Number-Shape, Number-Rhyme, Roman Room and Alphabet Systems.

Each of the five systems can be used either independently or in conjunction with another system. Furthermore, one or two of the systems of your choice can be set aside, if you wish, as 'constant memory banks' if you have certain lists or orders of items that you will need to be able to recall over a period of a year or more.

Before moving on to the broader systems, however, I want to introduce you to a simple and intriguing method for instantly doubling the capacity of any of the systems you have learned so far. When you have reached the end of a system but wish to add further associations, all you have to do is to go back to the beginning of your system and imagine your association word exactly as you usually imagine it, but as if it were contained in a huge block of ice. This simple visualisation technique will drastically change the association pictures you have formed and will double the effectiveness of your system by giving you the original list plus that list in its new context.

For example, if your first key in the Number-Shape System was *paintbrush*, you would imagine that same paintbrush either buried in the heart of your giant block of ice or protruding from the corners or sides. If your first word in the Number-Rhyme System was *bun*, then you could imagine a hot bun melting the edges of the ice block in which it was contained. If your first word in the

Alphabet System was *ace*, then you could imagine a giant playing card either frozen in the centre or forming one of the six sides of the ice block. If, therefore, you were using your 'second' Alphabet System (the alphabet in a huge block of ice), and the first item you wanted to remember was *parrot*, you might imagine your parrot crashing through the centre heart, spade, club or diamond of your card, shattering, with lots of squawking and cracking, the ice block.

Onword

You now have the ability to remember randomly linked items, two sets of ten items, a large number of ordered items (your Roman Room), and 26 ordered items. And you can instantly double that capacity by using the 'block of ice' method.

Your
Memory's
Rhythms

11

Preview
- Recall During a Learning Period
- Recall During Learning Memory Test
- Recall After Learning

In addition to the SMASHIN' SCOPE Memory Principles you are applying throughout this book, there are two major areas that, if you understand them, will enable you to double the efficiency of your memory while you are taking in information and then to double it again after you have taken the information in: (1) recall during learning; and (2) recall after learning.

Recall During a Learning Period

In order for you to see clearly how your memory rhythms function during a standard learning period, it will be useful for you to experience a brief 'recall during a learning period' yourself. To do this, follow these instructions carefully: read the long list of words overleaf, one word at a time, once only, *without using any memory systems or techniques, and without going back over any words*. The purpose of your reading the list will be to see how many of the words you can remember without using any of the Memory Principles. When you are reading the list, simply try to remember as many of the words in order as you can. Start reading down the columns now, and then test yourself.

was	the	range
away	of	of
left	beyond	and
two	Leonardo da Vinci	and
his	which	else
and	the	the
the	must	walk
far	and	room
of	of	finger
and	could	small
that	the	change

Recall During Learning Memory Test

Now that you have completed reading the list cover it up and write down below as many of the words as possible.

Now check the way in which your own memory worked: as a general principle, people remember more of what they learn at the beginning and end of a learning period, many more things that were associated with each other, and always more items that stand out in some way.

Thus, the words in this test that are commonly remembered are the first three to five words; the last two or three words; *and, of* and *the* (remembered because of repetition and linking to themselves), and *Leonardo da Vinci*, because it stands out from the rest. In addition, people will remember their own specially associated groups of words within the list, as well as words that for some personal reason are outstanding to them.

It is important to observe what was not remembered: *anything* that was not at the beginning or end of the learning period, that was not associated with other parts of the learning period, and that was not in any way outstanding. In many cases, this means that the entire bulk of the middle section of the learning period can be forgotten. Relating all of this to yourself and to time, ask yourself the following question: if you had been studying a difficult text for forty minutes, had found your understanding fairly poor throughout, and had noticed that during the last ten minutes of your reading your understanding had begun to improve slightly, would you: (a) stop studying immediately and conclude that as you had started to do well you could now stop and have a rest; or (b) carry on, assuming that now your understanding was flowing more smoothly, you'd be able to keep it going until it trailed off, and *then* take your break?

Most people choose the latter of these two alternatives, assuming that if their understanding is going well all other things will also be going well. It can, however, be seen from the results of the test you have just taken, and from your own personal experience, that understanding and recall are *not* the same. They vary in amounts enormously, and the factor that defines their difference is your own time management.

What you understand you do not necessarily recall, and as time progresses while you learn, you will recall less and less of what you are understanding if you do not in some way solve the problem of the large dip in recall that occurs during the middle of the learning period (*see graph page 82*). This Memory Rhythm applies no matter what you are learning, and that includes the learning of memory systems. What you are looking for is a learning situation in which both recall and understanding can work in maximum harmony.

You can create this situation only by organising the time in which you are learning in such a way as to enable understanding to remain high without giving the memory a chance to sag too deeply in the middle. This is easily accomplished by learning to divide your learning periods into the most beneficial time units. These units, on the average, turn out to be between 10 and 50 minutes, for example, 30 minutes, as shown in the graph on the next page. If your time is organised in this way, several advantages immediately become apparent:

1   Each of the inevitable dips in your memory during learning will not be as deep as if you had carried on without the break.
2   Instead of only two high points of recall at the beginning and end of the learning period, you will have as many as eight 'beginning and ending' high points of recall.

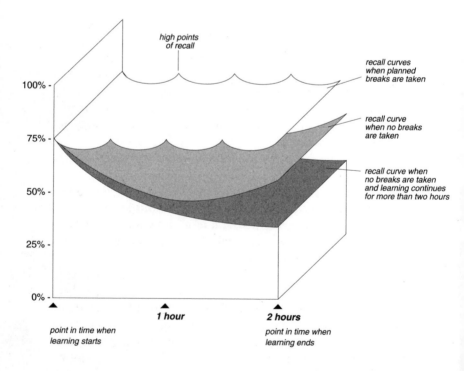

A graph showing which time units give maximum recall.

3 Because you are taking breaks, you will be far more rested during your next learning period than you would have been had you continued to work without breaks. The additional advantage of this is that when you are rested, both recall *and* understanding function more easily and efficiently.

4 Because when you are taking breaks you are both more rested and recalling more of each learning session, your comprehension of the next new section in which you find yourself after the break will be greater because you will have laid a firmer foundation in which to nourish and associate the new information. The person who has not taken such breaks, in addition to a growing fatigue, will be recalling less of what he has learned before, and therefore will be able to make continually fewer and fewer connections between the dwindling amount of information he has learned and the increasingly formidable and non-understandable information that threatens him.

5 Contrary to 'common sense', your memory of what you have learned *rises* during the breaks you take rather than immediately beginning to fall. This rise is due to the fact that your left and right hemispheres 'sort things out' for a little while on an unconscious level after you have finished taking in information during a learning period. When you return to your learning after the break you are therefore actually in possession of *more* conscious knowledge than if you had carried on without the break. This last piece of information is particularly important because it dispels those deep feelings of guilt that you may experience when you find yourself naturally taking a break but at the same time thinking that you ought to be getting 'back to the grindstone'. (*See* Use Your Head – *details in chapter 9, page 114.*)

Your breaks should usually be no longer than two to ten minutes. During each break you can allow your mind to rest by going for a short walk, making yourself a light non-alcoholic drink, doing some form of physical exercise, auto-suggesting, meditating, or listening to quiet music.

To consolidate and improve your memory even further, it is advisable at the beginning and end of each learning period to perform a very quick review and preview of what you have learned in the previous learning periods and what you are going to learn in the coming ones. This continuing review/preview cycle helps to further consolidate the information you already have, gives you growing confidence and success as you progress, allows your mind to direct itself toward the next learning target, and gives you a bird's-eye view of the territory you are going to explore mentally during your entire learning session.

Combining your knowledge of the rhythms of your memory in time during a learning period with the Memory Principles and using your creative imagination, you will be able to form imaginative links and associations throughout your period of study, consequently transforming the sags in the middle of the learning periods into nearly straight lines.

Recall After Learning

Once you have made it easier for your recall to work well during a learning period, it is important for you to do the same thing for your recall after the learning period. The pattern of recall after learning contains two 'surprises': first, you retain more of what you have learned *after* a few minutes have passed since the end of your learning period; second, you lose 80 per cent of the detail you have learned within 24 hours of having learned it. (You can make use of this dramatic fall to help you 'take the coats off' your 'memory coat hangers' as discussed in chapter 6.) The rise is beneficial, so you want to make use of it; the decline can be disastrous, so you usually need to make sure that it does not happen. The method for both maintaining the rise and preventing the decline is Review with Repetition.

If you have been studying for one hour, the high point in your recall after learning will occur approximately ten minutes afterwards. This high point is the ideal time for your first review. The function of your review is to imprint the information you already have in your mind, in order to make it more 'solid'. If you manage to review at the first high point, the graph of recall after learning changes, and instead of the detailed information being lost to recall, it is maintained, as shown in the graph on page 87. For example, if you had studied for one hour, your first review would take place after ten minutes and your second review would take place 24 hours later. From then on, your review should take place as indicated on page 87. On average, these reviews all occur over units of time that are based on calendar elements, i.e., days, weeks, months, years. So, you would review after one day, then after one week, then after one month, then after half a year, and so on.

Each review need take very little time. The first one should consist of reviewing your Mind Map Memory Notes (*see chapter 22, page 143*) of information after the learning period. This may take as much as ten minutes for a one-hour learning period. After the first review, each subsequent review should consist of a quick jotting down of the basic information in your area of interest, and then a comparison of your quick notes with your basic notes. Any areas you have missed out can be filled in, and any new knowledge you may have acquired during the period between reviews can be added to your marginal notes. In this manner, your recall of all the information that you need to have constantly available can be guaranteed.

It is useful to compare the minds of people who consistently review with the minds of those who do not. People who do not review are continually putting information in and letting that same information drain out. These people will constantly find it difficult to take in new information because the background knowledge they need to understand that new information will have gone. In such a case, learning will continually be difficult, recall will always be inadequate, and the whole process of learning, understanding and recall will be unpleasant and arduous.

People who *do* review will find that with the constantly available store of increasing information, new information will slot in more easily. This will create a positive cycle in which learning, understanding and recall assist one another, making the continuing process increasingly easy.

Surprisingly, the more you learn the easier it is for you to learn more. It is similar to the biblical phrase, 'To him that hath shall be given, but from him that hath not, even that little which he hath shall be taken away.'

This information on recall after learning can also be applied to our current attitudes towards the decline of mental abilities, especially memory, with age. All our current statistics indicate that as human beings grow older their memories become increasingly worse after the age of 24. These findings, substantial as they seem, contain a major fault. They are based on surveys that studied people who generally did not have any information about how their memories worked and who consequently tended to neglect them. In other words, the tests showing that human memory declines with age were performed on people who consistently did not use the Memory Principles and did not review what they had learned. They therefore fell into the second category of the biblical statement.

Recent experiments on people who have applied the Memory Principles and who have properly managed their memory rhythms during and after learning have shown that the *opposite* of the established findings are in fact the case. If you continue to use the numerical, linguistic, analytical, logical and sequential abilities of the left side of your brain, and if you continue to use the rhythmical, musical, imaginative, colourful and dimensional abilities of the right side of your brain, along with the Memory Principles and Memory Time Rhythm – all in a continual self-educating approach – your memory will not only not decline with age but will actually improve enormously. The more it is fed, the more it will enable you to build up **imaginative** and **associative** networks with new areas of knowledge, and thus the more it will be able to both remember and create.

Onword

The more you give to your memory, then, the more your memory will give back to you, and with compound interest.

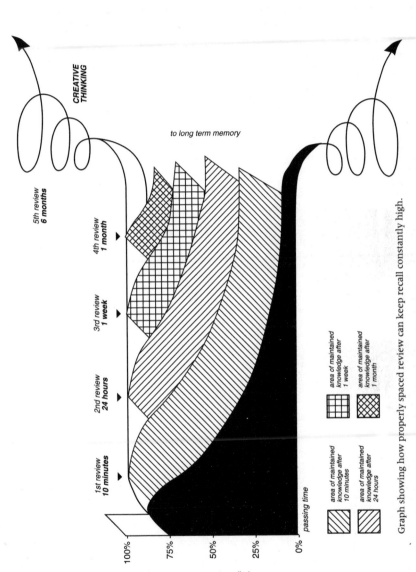

Graph showing how properly spaced review can keep recall constantly high.

Part Two

Memory

the Major System

The Major System

Preview
- The Major System's Special Code
- Initial Major System Exercise

Having enormously increased the flexibility of your mind, your abilities to imagine, associate, sense and create are ready to take on and easily master the Major System, a system that can be used to create – should you so wish – limitless memory systems!

The Major System is the ultimate Basic Memory System. It has been used and continually improved upon for more than 300 years, since the middle of the seventeenth century, when it was introduced by Stanislaus Mink von Wennsshein. It was devised to enable the master memorisers of the time to break the bonds of the previously excellent but more limited systems. These master memorisers wanted a system that would enable them to memorise a list of items not only longer than ten but as long as they wanted. At the same time they wanted this system to enable them to remember numbers and dates and to order and structure memory in hundreds and thousands of detailed ways.

The basic concept of the system is that it makes use of a different consonant or consonant sound for each number from 0 to 9 in a special code:

The Major System's Special Code

Number = associated code

- 0 = *s, z,* soft *c*
- 1 = *d, t, th*
- 2 = *n*
- 3 = *m*
- 4 = *r*
- 5 = *l*
- 6 = *j, sh,* soft *ch, dg,* soft *g*
- 7 = *k,* hard *ch,* hard *c,* hard *g, ng, qu*
- 8 = *f, v*
- 9 = *b, p*

The vowels *a, e, i, o, u* and the letters *h, w* and *y* do not have numbers associated with them and are used simply as 'blanks' in the Key Memory Image Words you will soon be creating.

To save you the trouble of remembering these by rote, there are some simple remembering devices:

0   The letter *s,* or *z,* is the first sound of the word *zero,* *o* is the last letter.

1   The letters *d* and *t* have one downstroke.

2   The letter *n* has two downstrokes.

3   The letter *m* has three downstrokes.

4   The letter *r* is the last letter in the word *four.*

5   The letter *l* can be thought of as either the Roman numeral for 50 or an open hand, the index finger and thumb forming an L shape.

6   The letter *j* is the mirror image of 6.

7   The letter *k,* when seen as a capital, contains two number 7s.

8   The letter *f,* when handwritten, has two loops, similar to the number 8.

9   The letters *b* and *p* are the mirror image of 9.

As with the Number-Rhyme and Number-Shape Systems, your task is to create a Key Image Word that can be immediately and permanently linked with the number it represents. Take, for example, the number 1. You have to think of a Key Image Word that is a good visual image and that contains only *d, t* or *th* and a vowel sound. Examples include *day, tea, toe* and *the.* When recalling the word chosen for number 1, let us say day, you would know that it could represent only the number 1 because the consonant letter in the word represents no other number, and vowels do not count as numbers in this system.

Try another example: the number 34. In this case the number 3 is represented by the letter *m*, and 4 is represented by the letter *r*. Examples of possible words include *mare*, *more*, *moor* and *mire*. In selecting the 'best' word for this number, you once again make use of the alphabet order to assist both in choice of word and in recall: in other words, the letters you have to choose are *m* and *r*, so you simply mentally run through the vowels *a-e-i-o-u* using the *first* vowel that enables you to make an adequate Memory Word. The case in question is easily solved, since *a* fits between *m* and *r* to direct you toward the word *mare*.

The advantage of using this alphabet order system is that, should a word in the Major System ever be forgotten, it can actually be 'worked out' from the basic information. All you have to do is place the letters of the number in their correct order and then 'slot in', in order, the vowels. As soon as you touch the correct combination, your Key Memory Image Word will immediately come to mind.

First, letting the letter *d* represent in each case the '1' of the number, try to complete the words for numbers 10 to 19, using the alphabet order system for these numbers, in the Initial Major System Exercise below.

Don't worry if this exercise proves a little difficult, because overleaf is a complete list of Memory Words for the numbers 0 to 100. Don't just accept them: check each one carefully, changing any that you find difficult to visualise or for which you have a better substitute.

Use a strong noun or verb as it creates a good Memory Image on which to hang your information.

Initial Major System Exercise

Number	Letters	Word
10	d a z e	daze
11	d d	dad / den
12	d n	dam
13	n	dare—
14	R	dale
15	L	
16	J	dj —
17	K	duke -
18	F	deaf—
19	b/p	dub

The Major System – Initial 101 Key Words

0	Saw	34	Mare	68	Chaff
1	Day	35	Mail	69	Chap
2	Noah	36	Mash	70	Case
3	Ma	37	Mac	71	Cat
4	Ra	38	Mafia	72	Can
5	Law	39	Map	73	Cameo
6	Jaw	40	Race	74	Car
7	Key	41	Rat	75	Call
8	Fee	42	Rain	76	Cage
9	Bay	43	Ram	77	Cake
10	Daze	44	Ra-ra	78	Café
11	Dad	45	Rail	79	Cab
12	Dan	46	Rage	80	Face
13	Dam	47	Rack	81	Fad
14	Dairy	48	Rafia	82	Fan
15	Dale	49	Rap	83	Fame
16	Dash	50	Lace	84	Fair
17	Deck	51	Lad	85	Fall
18	Daffy	52	Lane	86	Fish
19	Dab	53	Lamb	87	Fag
20	NASA	54	Lair	88	Fife
21	Net	55	Lily	89	Fab
22	Nan	56	Lash	90	Base
23	Name	57	Lake	91	Bat
24	Nero	58	Lava	92	Ban
25	Nail	59	Lab	93	Bam!
26	Niche	60	Chase	94	Bar
27	Nag	61	Chat	95	Ball
28	Navy	62	Chain	96	Bash
29	Nab	63	Chime	97	Back
30	Mace	64	Chair	98	Beef
31	Mat	65	Cello	99	Babe
32	Man	66	Cha-cha	100	Daisies
33	Ma'am	67	Check		

You now possess the code and keys to a Peg Memory System for the numbers from 0 to 100 – a system that contains the pattern for its own memorisation. As you have seen, this system is basically limitless. In other words, now that you have letters for the numbers 0 to 9, it should be possible for you to devise Key Image Words for the numbers not only from 0 to 100 but also from 100 to 1000. This system could of course go on forever. For those of you who wish to do this, I have developed a system named SEM[3] (the Self-Enhancing Master Memory Matrix), which is outlined in detail in my book *Master Your Memory*.

An alternative method is to 'stick with' the method of making every number into a letter, and making a Key Memory Image Word from that combination of letters.

On the pages that follow I have devised a list of Key Image Words for the numbers 100 to 1000. After certain of the more difficult words I have included: (1) a suggestion for a way in which an image might be formed from the word; or (2) a dictionary definition of the word, the definition including words or ideas that should help you form your image; or (3) 'new' definitions for words that place them in a humorous or unusual but certainly more memorable form.

The remaining words are followed by blank spaces. In the space provided you should write in your own Key Words for, or ideas about, the image you will be using. In some cases, where the combination of letters makes the use of single words impossible, double words have been used, such as *no cash* for the number 276 (*n*, hard *c*, *sh*). In other cases it is necessary to include vowels (which have no numerical meaning) at the beginning of the word. For example, the number 394 (*m, p, r*) is represented by the word *empire*. In still other cases, words have been used of which the first three letters only pertain to the number. For example, the number 359 (*m, 1, b*) is represented by the word *mailbag*. The final *g* is ignored.

If you wish to expand Your Major System beyond 100, your next task is to check this Major System list carefully. It would obviously be too much to ask you to do this at one sitting, so I suggest the more modest goal of checking, making images for, and remembering ten items each day. As you go through the list, attempt to make your images of the words as solid as you can. Remember that as you memorise this entire list, you should try to use both sides of your cortex, making sure that you are reviewing and consolidating the order, while at the same time increasing and expanding your imagination, your creativity, and your awareness of your senses.

Even when words refer to ideas or concepts, bring them down to a more concrete level. For example, the number 368, represented by the Memory Words *much force*, should not be pictured as some vague power or energy in space but should be visualised as an image in which much force is used to accomplish or destroy – for example, a weight-lifter at the Olympics. In other words, in each case you will be attempting to make the Memory Word as pictorial and as memorable as possible. Remember the rules in chapter 5: use your whole SMASHIN' SCOPE.

In cases where words are similar in concept to previous words, it is most important to make your images as different as possible. The same caution applies to words that are pluralised because of the addition of *s*. In these cases, imagine a great number of items as opposed to one enormous item. You will find your consolidation of the words in the Major System useful not only because it will enable you to remember the astounding number of 1000 items (in order or randomly) but also because it will exercise your creative linking ability, which is so necessary for remembering anything.

A number of the words used as mnemonics in this Major System are interesting in their own right. As you check through and memorise each list of 100, have a dictionary by your side, for help if you run into difficulty selecting your Key Words. In these instances, it will serve as a means of solidifying the images for you, will enable you to select the best possible images or words, and will be of value in the improvement of your general vocabulary. If you have read my book *The Speed Reading Book*, combine, where feasible, the vocabulary exercises included in it with your exercises on the Major System.

101 Dust
102 Design
103 Dismay
104 Desire
105 Dazzle
106 Discharge
107 Disc
108 Deceive
109 Despair
110 Dates – succulent sticky fruit
111 Deadwood – decayed. often twisted, remains of trees
112 Deaden
113 Diadem – a crown; a wreath of leaves or flowers worn around the head
114 Daughter
115 Detail
116 Detach
117 Toothache
118 Dative – a noun case that expresses giving
119 Deathbed
120 Tennis
121 Dent
122 Denun – to take a nun or nuns away from a place or situation
123 Denim
124 Dinner
125 Downhill
126 Danish – native to Denmark
127 Dank – unpleasantly soaked or damp; marshy or swampy
128 Downfall
129 Danube – the river(or picture waltzing to the *Blue Danube)*
130 Demise
131 Domed – having a large, rounded summit, as a head or a church
132 Demon
133 Demimonde – the fringe of society
134 Demure
135 Dimly
136 Damage
137 Democracy
138 Dam full
139 Damp
140 Dress
141 Dart
142 Drain
143 Dram
144 Drawer
145 Drill
146 Dredge – apparatus for bringing up mud (or oysters) from the sea or river bottom
147 Drag
148 Drive
149 Drip
150 De luxe
151 Daylight
152 Delinquent
153 Dilemma – a position leaving a choice that is usually between two evils
154 Dealer
155 Delilah – temptress of Samson; false and wily woman
156 Deluge – a great flood; Noah's flood

157   Delicacy
158   Delphi – the ancient Greek town where the sanctuary of the oracle was located
159   Tulip
160   Duchess
161   Dashed
162   Dudgeon – state of strong anger, resentment, or feeling of offence
163   Dutchman
164   Dodger – a wily, tricky, elusive person
165   Dash light – imagine the dash light in your car
166   Dishwasher
167   Dechoke – reverse the image of choke, either in relation to a car or to strangling someone
168   Dishevel – to make the hair or clothes loose, disordered, 'flung about'
169   Dish up – to serve food, usually applied to a slapdash manner
170   Decks
171   Decade
172   Token
173   Decamp – imagine confusion in the dismantling of tents, etc.
174   Decree – an order made by an authority demanding some kind of action
175   Ducal – imagine anything similar to or looking like a duke
176   Duckish
177   Decaying
178   Take-off
179   Decapitate
180   Defact
181   Defeat
182   Divan
183   Defame
184   Diver
185   Defile
186   Devotion
187   Edifying
188   Two frisky fillies – imagine them in a field or memorable enclosure
189   Two frightened boys – perhaps being chased by 188!
190   Debase – to lower in character, quality or value
191   Debate
192   Debone – to pick the bones out of, usually from fish
193   Whitebeam – a tree with long, silvery underleaves
194   Dipper – imagine a big dipper at a fairground
195   Dabble
196   Debauch
197   Dipping – imagine someone being dipped forcibly into water, as the medieval torture
198   Dab off – imagine a stain or blood being

Plate I The Link System – imagination, exaggeration, absurdity, association, colour . . .
See pages 49 to 51.

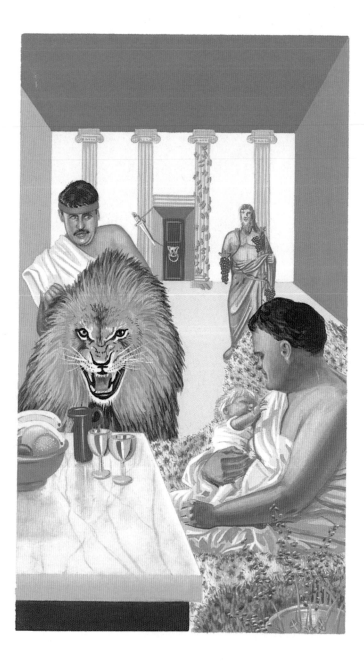

Plate II An example of the Roman Room System. *See pages 67 to 69.*

Plate III A Mind Map which summarises this book. *See pages 143 to 144.*

Plate IV An example of dream memorisation showing the Key Main Images. *See pages 179 to 181.*

The Major System   97

'dabbed off' with
cotton wool
199 Depip – to take the pips
out of (imagine a
pomegranate)
200 Nieces
201 Nasty
202 Insane
203 Noisome – harmful,
noxious, ill-smelling
204 No Sir!
205 Nestle
206 Incision – a clean
cutting of something,
as with a doctor's
scalpel
207 Nosegay – a small
bunch of sweet-
scented flowers
208 Unsafe
209 Newsboy
210 Notice
211 Needed
212 Indian
213 Anatomy
214 Nadir – the lowest
point; place or time of
great depression
215 Needle
216 Night watch
217 Antique
218 Native
219 Antibes – a port and
resort in south-east
France, on the
Mediterranean
220 Ninnies – group of
people with weak
minds, simpletons
221 Ninth – imagine the
ninth hole of a golf
course

222 Ninon – a lightweight
dress fabric made of
silk
223 No name – imagine a
person who has
forgotten his name
224 Nunnery
225 Union hall
226 Nunnish – pertaining
to or like a nun
227 Non-aqua – having
nothing at all to do
with water
228 Nineveh
229 Ninepin – one of nine
upright pieces of wood
to be knocked down in
the game of ninepins
230 Names
231 Nomad
232 Nominee – a person
nominated for a
position or office
233 No ma'am
234 Enamour – to charm,
to animate with love
235 Animal
236 No mash – imagine a
saucepan that has just
been emptied of
mashed potatoes
237 Unmake
238 Nymph – a beautiful
mythological maiden,
always young
239 Numb
240 Nurse
241 Narrate
242 No run
243 Norm – a standard; a
set pattern to be
maintained

244 Narrower
245 Nearly
246 Nourish
247 New York
248 Nerve
249 Nearby
250 Nails
251 Nailed
252 Nylon
253 New loam – freshly turned rich and fertile soil
254 Kneeler
255 Nail hole
256 Knowledge
257 Nailing
258 Nullify
259 Nail-brush
260 Niches – vertical recesses in a wall to contain a statue
261 Unshod
262 Nation
263 Unjam
264 Injure
265 Unshell – to extract a living organism from its shell
266 Nosh shop – imagine a corner snack-bar or something similar
267 No joke – a joke that falls flat
268 Unshaved
269 Unship – imagine a great crowd of people being ordered off a ship
270 Necks
271 Naked
272 Noggin – a small mug and/or its contents
273 Income

274 Anchor
275 Nickel – a grey metal related to cobalt
276 No cash – imagine someone fumbling in his pockets in order to pay a restaurant bill
277 Knocking
278 Encave – to confine to a dark place; to keep in a cave
279 Uncap – imagine schoolboys stealing one another's caps
280 Nephews
281 Nevada
282 Uneven
283 Infamy
284 Never
285 Navel
286 Knavish – having the characteristics of a roguish trickster
287 Invoke – to address in prayer; to implore assistance or protection
288 Unfavourable
289 Enfeeble – to make extremely weak and unable to function
290 Nibs
291 Unpod – to take from the pod, as peas
292 New pan – imagine a brilliantly shiny frying pan
293 New beam – imagine the first beam ever from the sun
294 Neighbour
295 Nibble
296 Nippish

297	Unpack	327	Maniac
298	Unpaved	328	Manful – brave, resolute, bold
299	Nabob – a wealthy person, especially one returned from India with a fortune	329	Monopoly – a popular board game
300	Moses	330	Maims
301	Mast	331	Mammoth
302	Mason	332	Mammon – the Syrian god of riches; worldly wealth
303	Museum	333	My mum
304	Miser	334	Memory
305	Missile	335	Mammal
306	Massage	336	My match
307	Mask	337	Mimic
308	Massive	338	Mummify – to preserve the body by embalming
309	Mishap	339	Mump
310	Midas – the king who turned everything he touched to gold	340	Mars
311	Midday	341	Maraud – to make a plunderous raid; to go about pilfering
312	Maiden	342	Marine
313	Madam	343	Miriam
314	Motor	344	Mirror
315	Medal	345	Moral
316	Modish – in the current style or fashion	346	March
317	Medic	347	Mark
318	Midwife	348	Morphia – the principal narcotic of opium
319	Mudpie	349	Marble
320	Manse – the home of a Presbyterian minister	350	Males
321	Mend	351	Malt
322	Minion – favourite child, servant or animal; slave	352	Melon
323	Minim – a creature of the smallest size or importance; a musical note	353	Mile man – a man who runs a mile
		354	Miller
		355	Molehill
324	Manner	356	Mulish – imagine anything that is characteristic of a mule
325	Manila		
326	Manage		

357 Milk
358 Mollify – to soften, assuage, appease
359 Mailbag
360 Matches
361 Mashed
362 Machine
363 Mishmash – a jumble, hotchpotch, medley
364 Major
365 Mesh lock – imagine something like a gear cog meshing and locking or a lock that operates by an intricate mesh
366 Magician
367 Magic
368 Much force
369 Much bent
370 Mikes
371 Mocked
372 Mohican
373 Make muck
374 Maker
375 Meekly
376 My cash
377 Making
378 Make off – to hurry away, as a thief from the scene of a crime
379 Magpie
380 Mauve skirt
381 Mufti – an expounder of Mohammedan law; civilian dress as opposed to uniform
382 Muffin
383 Movement
384 Mayfair
385 Muffle

386 My fish
387 Mafeking a town in South Africa, well known for relief of siege there in 1900
388 Mauve feet
389 Movable
390 Mopes – sulks; being dull or out of spirits
391 Moped
392 Embank – to confine or protect (river, road, etc.) by a bank
393 Wampum – name for money beads and shells used by North American Indians
394 Empire
395 Maple
396 Ambush
397 Impact
398 Mob violence
399 Imbibe – to drink in; absorb (often used of liquor)
400 Recess
401 Recite
402 Raisin
403 Résumé – a summing up; a condensed statement; a summary
404 Racer
405 Wrestle
406 Rose show
407 Risk
408 Receive
409 Rasp – to rub with a coarse file; to utter in a grating way
410 Raids
411 Radiate

412 Rattan – Indian climbing palm with a long, thin, pliable stem

413 Redeem

414 Radar – imagine 'beaming in' on some object in the sky

415 Rattle

416 Radish

417 Reading

418 Ratify – to settle, confirm, approve, establish

419 Rat bait

420 Reigns

421 Rained

422 Reunion

423 Uranium – a radioactive white metallic element

424 Runner

425 Runnel – a rivulet or gutter

426 Ranch

427 Rank

428 Run-off – a decisive final contest; a gutter or spillway

429 Rainbow

430 Remus – one of two brothers suckled by a wolf in infancy; he became one of the mythological founders of Rome

431 Rammed

432 Roman

433 Remember

434 Ramrod

435 Rommel – notorious German war leader

436 Rummage

437 Remake

438 Ramify – to form branches, subdivisions or offshoots

439 Ramp

440 Roars

441 Reared

442 Rareness

443 Rear man – the last man in a column or file

444 Rarer

445 Rarely

446 Raree show – a peepshow

447 Rearing

448 Rarefy – to lessen the density or solidity of, especially air

449 Rarebit – a dainty morsel; often applied to Welsh rarebit

450 Release

451 Railed

452 Reloan

453 Realm

454 Roller

455 Reel line – imagine a fishing line tangled on its reel

456 Relish

457 Relic

458 Relief

459 Relapse

460 Riches

461 Reached

462 Region

463 Regime – mode, style, diet; form of government

464 Rasher

465 Rachel

466 Rejudge

467 Raging

468 Arch foe – imagine yourself as a knight with one giant foe among a number of others

469 Reach up

470 Racks

471 Racket

472 Reckon

473 Requiem – a service spoken or sung for the peace of the soul of a dead person

474 Raker – imagine a man who does nothing but rake gardens

475 Recall

476 Roguish

477 Rococo – a highly ornamental, florid style in design

478 Recover

479 Rack up – colloquialism meaning to score points in sport

480 Refuse

481 Raft

482 Raven

483 Revamp – to renovate, revise or improve

484 Reefer – a marijuana cigarette

485 Raffle

486 Ravage

487 Revoke – a card player's failure to follow suit, though he could

488 Revive

489 Rough passage – a crossing over rough sea; a difficult or testing time

490 Rabies

491 Rabid – furious, violent, unreasoning, mad

492 Ribbon

493 Ripe melon

494 Rapier

495 Rabble

496 Rubbish

497 Rebuke

498 Rebuff

499 Republic – a society with equality among members

500 Lasses

501 Last

502 Lesson

503 Lyceum – a place in Athens where Aristotle taught

504 Laser – a super-concentrated beam of light coming from a vibrating substance

505 Lazily

506 Alsatian

507 Lacing

508 Lucifer

509 Lisp

510 Ladies

511 Lighted

512 Latin

513 Late meal

514 Ladder

515 Ladle

516 Old age

517 Leading

518 Old foe

519 Lead pipe

520 Lance

521	Land	555	Lily-livered
522	Linen	556	Low ledge
523	Liniment	557	Lilac
524	Linear	558	Low life
525	Lineal	559	Lullaby
526	Launch	560	Lashes
527	Lank	561	Legit – colloquial for that which is honest
528	Lunar flight		
529	Line-up	562	Legion
530	Looms	563	Lush meadow
531	Limit	564	Lecher
532	Layman	565	Lushly
533	Lame mare	566	All-Jewish
534	Lamarck – famous French zoologist and botanist	567	Logic
		568	Low shove
		569	Lush pea
535	Lamella – a thin plate, especially of tissue or bone	570	Lakes
		571	Licked
		572	Lagoon
536	Lime juice	573	Locum – colloquial for a deputy in any office, especially a doctor
537	Looming		
538	Lymph – a bodily fluid resembling plasma		
		574	Lacquer
539	Lamp	575	Local
540	Layers	576	Luggage
541	Lard	577	Licking
542	Learn	578	Liquefy – to bring a solid or a gas to a liquid condition
543	Alarm		
544	Leerer		
545	Laurel	579	Lock-up
546	Large	580	Leaves
547	Lark	581	Livid
548	Larva	582	Elfin – like, or relating to, a fairy or an elf
549	Larrup – colloquial for 'to thrash'		
		583	Alluvium – soil deposited or washed down by the action of water
550	Lilies		
551	Lilt		
552	Lowland		
553	Lilo mattress – a camping mattress that serves as a bed	584	Lever
		585	Level
		586	Lavish
554	Lowlier	587	Leaving

588   Leave off
589   Lifeboat
590   Lips
591   Leaped
592   Lib now – imagine this phrase as a women's liberation placard
593   Low bum
594   Labour
595   Label
596   Lip chap – a cold sore on the lip
597   Lawbook
598   Leapfrog
599   Lap up
600   Chases
601   Chaste
602   Jason – and the Golden Fleece
603   Chessman
604   Chaser
605   Chisel
606   Cheese show
607   Chasing
608   Joseph
609   Cheese pie
610   Shades
611   Shaded
612   Showdown
613   Chatham – naval dockyard town on the River Medway, Kent
614   Chatter
615   Chattel
616   Chitchat
617   Cheating
618   Shadoof – a mechanism for raising water, consisting of a long pole hung from a post, and a bucket, used in Egypt
619   Chat up – to talk to a person of the opposite sex with further contact in mind
620   Chains
621   Chant
622   Genuine
623   Chinaman
624   Joiner
625   Channel
626   Change
627   Chink – in the armour
628   Geneva – headquarters for certain United Nations organisations; major city of Switzerland
629   Shinbone
630   Chums
631   Ashamed
632   Showman
633   Jemima – boot with elastic sides, having no laces or clasps to fasten
634   Chimera – a fire-breathing monster with a lion's head, a goat's body and a dragon's tail; a fanciful product of the imagination
635   Shameless
636   Jimjams – nervous fears; delirium tremens
637   Jamaica
638   Shameful
639   Champ
640   Cheers
641   Chart
642   Shrine
643   Chairman
644   Juror

645 Churl – a surly, ill-bred man
646 Charge
647 Cherokee – North American Indian
648 Giraffe
649 Chirp
650 Jealous
651 Child
652 Chilean
653 Shalom salutation at meeting or parting, used by Jews
654 Jailer
655 Shallowly – in a manner not intellectual or lacking in depth
656 Geology
657 Gelignite
658 Shelf
659 Julep – with mint
660 Judges
661 Judged
662 Jejune – bare, meagre, empty; void of interest
663 Judgement
664 Judger
665 Jewishly
666 Choo-choo-choo – an especially puffy steam engine
667 Joshing – good-natured leg pulling or joking
668 Jehoshaphat – a king of Judah
669 Shoe shop
670 Checks
671 Checked
672 Chicken
673 Checkmate – a position in chess in which the opponent's king is trapped; the end of the game
674 Checker
675 Chuckle
676 Check shirt
677 Checking
678 Chekhov – famous Russian author of plays and short stories
679 Jacob
680 Chafes – makes sore or worn by rubbing; irritates
681 Shaft
682 Shaven
683 Chief Mohawk
684 Shaver
685 Joyful
686 Chiffchaff – small European warbler with yellowish-brown plumage
687 Chafing
688 Shove off
689 Shavable
690 Chaps
691 Chapter
692 Japan
693 Jobman
694 Chopper
695 Chapel
696 Sheepish
697 Chipping
698 Sheepfold
699 Shopboy
700 Kisses
701 Cast
702 Casino
703 Chasm

704 Kisser
705 Gazelle
706 Kiss-shy – reluctant to kiss
707 Cask
708 Cohesive – with the quality of sticking together
709 Cusp – the point at which two branches of a curve meet and stop; a pointed end, especially of a crescent moon
710 Cats
711 Cadet
712 Cotton
713 Gotham – a proverbially foolish town
714 Guitar
715 Cattle
716 Cottage
717 Coating
718 Cadaver – a corpse
719 Cut up
720 Cans
721 Canada
722 Cannon
723 Economy
724 Coiner
725 Kennel
726 Conjurer
727 Conk – colloquial for 'to bang on the head'
728 Convey
729 Canopy – a covering over a bed or a throne
730 Cameos – pieces of relief carving in stone and agate, etc., with colour layers utilised to give background

731 Comet
732 Common
733 Commemorate
734 Camera
735 Camel
736 Game show – as seen on television
737 Comic
738 Comfy
739 Camp
740 Caress
741 Card
742 Corn
743 Cram
744 Career
745 Carol
746 Crash
747 Crack
748 Carafe – a glass water or wine bottle for the dinner table
749 Carp – to find fault; a freshwater fish
750 Class
751 Clod
752 Clan
753 Clam
754 Clear
755 Galileo – Italian astronomer, mathematician and physicist
756 Clash
757 Clack
758 Cliff
759 Clap
760 Cages
761 Caged
762 Cushion
763 Cashmere – a rich fabric or shawl,

originally made in
Kashmir, India

764 Cashier
765 Cajole – to persuade or
     soothe by flattery,
     deceit, etc.
766 Quiche shop
767 Catching
768 Cageful
769 Ketchup – tomato
     sauce
770 Cakes
771 Cooked
772 Cocoon
773 Cucumber
774 Cooker
775 Cackle
776 Quick change – rapid
     change of costume by
     an actor, etc., to play
     another part
777 Cooking
778 Quickfire
779 Cock-up – colloquial
     for that which has
     been made a mess of
780 Cafés
781 Cave-dweller
782 Coffin
783 Caveman
784 Caviar
785 Cavil – to raise
     needless objection
786 Coffee shop
787 Caving
788 Cavafy – poet of
     Alexandria
789 Coffee-bean
790 Cabs
791 Cupid
792 Cabin
793 Cabman

794 Caper – to frolic, skip,
     or leap lightly, as a
     lamb; a small berry
     used for making pickles
     and condiments
795 Cable
796 Cabbage
797 Coping
798 Keep off
799 Cobweb
800 Faces
801 Fast
802 Pheasant
803 Face mole
804 Visor
805 Facile
806 Visage
807 Facing
808 Face value
809 Face up – colloquial for
     'meet the brunt';
     accept the challenge or
     consequences
810 Fates – the three Greek
     goddesses of destiny
811 Faded
812 Fatten
813 Fathom
814 Fetter
815 Fatal
816 Fattish
817 Fading
818 Fateful
819 Football
820 Fans
821 Faint
822 Finance
823 Venom
824 Fawner – an
     obsequious or
     sycophantic person;

one who insincerely
praises for reward
825 Final
826 Finish
827 Fawning – courting
favour by cringing
828 Fanfare
829 Vain boy
830 Famous
831 Vomit
832 Famine
833 Fame-mad
834 Femur – the thigh-
bone
835 Female
836 Famish
837 Foaming
838 Fumeful
839 Vamp – adventuress;
woman who exploits
men; unscrupulous
flirt
840 Farce
841 Fort
842 Fern
843 Farm
844 Farrier – a man who
shoes horses or treats
them for disease
845 Frail
846 Fresh
847 Frock
848 Verify – establish the
truth of, bear out,
make good
849 Verb
850 False
851 Fault
852 Flan
853 Flame
854 Flare

855 Flail – wooden staff at
the end of which a
short heavy stick hangs
swinging; used for
threshing
856 Flash
857 Flake
858 Fluff
859 Flab
860 Fishes
861 Fished
862 Fashion
863 Fishmonger
864 Fisher
865 Facial
866 Fish shop
867 Fishing
868 Fish food
869 Fish bait
870 Focus
871 Faked
872 Fecund – fertile
873 Vacuum
874 Fakir – a
Mohammedan or
Hindu religious
devotee
875 Fickle
876 Fake china
877 Faking
878 Havocful – 'filled' with
devastation and
destruction
879 Vagabond
880 Fifes
881 Vivid
882 Vivien – Leigh
883 Five a m.
884 Fever
885 Favillous – consisting
of, or pertaining to,
ashes

886 Fifish – resembling or having the characteristics of a fife
887 Fifing
888 Vivify – give life to; enliven; animate
889 Viviparous – bringing forth live young rather than eggs
890 Fibs
891 Fibbed
892 Fabian – employing cautious strategy to wear out an enemy
893 Fob-maker
894 Fibre
895 Fable
896 Foppish
897 Fee back – imagine yourself receiving money you had paid for a product that was unsatisfactory
898 Few puffs – imagine someone trying to give up smoking
899 Fab boy – colloquialism for a young boy considered very attractive by girls
900 Basis
901 Pasta
902 Basin
903 Bosom
904 Bazaar
905 Puzzle
906 Beseech – to ask for earnestly; to entreat, supplicate or implore
907 Basic
908 Passive
909 Baseball

910 Beads
911 Bedded
912 Button
913 Bottom
914 Batter
915 Battle
916 Badge
917 Bedding
918 Beautify
919 Bad boy
920 Bans – curses; interdicts; prohibitions; sentences of outlawry
921 Band
922 Banana
923 Benumb – to make numb or torpid, insensible or powerless
924 Banner
925 Banal – trivial, trite, stale, commonplace
926 Banish
927 Bank
928 Banff – a holiday resort in north-east Scotland, in Grampian Region
929 Pin-up
930 Beams
931 Pomade – a scented ointment, originating from apples, for the hair
932 Bemoan – weep or express sorrow for or over; to lament or bewail
933 Beam-maker
934 Be merry
935 Pommel – a rounded knob, especially at the end of a sword-hilt
936 Bombshell

937   Beaming
938   Bumph – derogatory term for official documents, forms
939   Bump
940   Brass
941   Bread
942   Barn
943   Brim
944   Barrier
945   Barrel
946   Barge
947   Bark
948   Brief
949   Bribe
950   Blaze
951   Bald
952   Balloon
953   Blame
954   Boiler
955   Balliol – one of the Oxford colleges
956   Blush
957   Black
958   Bailiff – a king's representative in a district; agent or lord of a manor; officer under a sheriff
959   Bulb
960   Beaches
961   Budget
962   Passion
963   Pyjamas
964   Poacher – one who trespasses to steal game or fish; a vessel for poaching eggs
965   Bushel – an 8-gallon measure for grain and fruit
966   Push-chair
967   Bushwhacker – dweller in the backwoods
968   Bashful
969   Bishop
970   Bacchus – the Greek god of wine
971   Bucket
972   Bacon
973   Becalm – to still; to make quiet; delay through lack of wind, as a yacht
974   Baker
975   Buckle
976   Baggage
977   Backing – support, moral or physical; a web of strong material at the back of some woven fabric
978   Back off
979   Back up
980   Beehives
981   Buffet
982   Buffoon – a ludicrous figure; a droll clown
983   Pavement
984   Beaver
985   Baffle
986   Peevish – fretful or irritable
987   Bivouac – a temporary encampment without tents
988   Puffy face
989   Puff up
990   Babies
991   Puppet
992   Baboon
993   Pipe major
994   Paper
995   Babble

996   Baby show
997   Popgun
998   Pipeful
999   Pop-up – an automatic
        toaster; book with
        pages that rise when
        opened to give a three-
        dimensional effect
1000 These zoos

How to Increase by 1000 per cent

Everything You Have Learned So Far

13

It is possible, with ten quick leaps of your imagination, to create a memory system of 1000 from the basic 100 and a memory system of 10,000 from the basic 1000.

To achieve this, you use a similar method to that explained in chapter 10, which is simply to coat, cover or colour sections of your Major System in different substances, etc. For example, to expand the basic 100 words to 1000, using this new Multiplier Method, you would adjust the sections of your Major System as follows:

100–199	In a block of ice
200–299	Covered in thick oil
300–399	In flames
400–499	Coloured a brilliant and pulsating purple
500–599	Made of beautiful velvet
600–699	Completely transparent
700–799	Smelling of your favourite fragrance
800–899	Placed in the middle of a busy road
900–1000	Floating on a single cloud in a beautiful, sunny, clear sky

To multiply each of these ten 100s by 1000, thus giving you a total of 10,000, you use the same technique again. For example, by using the colours of the rainbow, you can bathe each of your 1000s in a different colour. Similarly, you could give each 1000 a different vision, or a different sound, or a different smell, or a different taste, or a different touch, or a different sensation. In these instances, the choice is up to you, and should be based on whatever gives you the strongest memory impressions.

For those interested in pursuing these Super-Memory systems further, see *Master Your Memory*. In that book, the Self-Enhancing Master Memory Matrix (SEM^3) outlines a complete system of 10,000 memory hooks, as well as providing 'key data' from the fields of art, music, literature, languages, geography, history, science and astronomy.

As with all previous systems, practise the Major System privately and with friends. You can probably already begin to sense that the memorisation of books, the preparation for examinations, and the like, are becoming increasingly easy tasks.

Onword

The applications of the Major System are almost as limitless as the System itself and later chapters in the book will show you how to apply it to the memorisation of cards, long numbers, telephone numbers, dates in history, birthdays and anniversaries, and information for examinations.

Card
Memory
System

Use the memory processes you have already learned to memorise a

complete pack of cards!

Magicians and memory experts often amaze and amuse audiences with their ability to remember complete packs of cards in the order in which they were presented. They similarly astound their audiences by being able to rattle off, without any difficulty, the six or seven cards not mentioned when an incomplete 'pack' is randomly presented. Extraordinary as these feats may seem, they are not all that difficult when using the memory processes you have already learned – even though many people accuse the performer of having hidden assistants in the audience, marked cards, and a number of other tricks.

The secret of remembering a complete pack of cards is to attach your Key Memory Image for each card to the Major System you have learned. All that is necessary to create a Key Memory Image Word for each card is to know the first letter of the word for the suit as well as the number of the card in that suit. For example, all words for the club cards will begin with *c*; all words for the hearts with *h*; all words for the spades with *s*; and all the words for the diamonds with *d*. The second consonant for the card-word will be the consonant represented by the letter from the Major System.

Taking as an example the 5 of spades, you know that it must begin with *s* because it is a spade card, and that its last consonant must be *l* because it is the 5, and 5 in the Major System is represented by *l*. Without much difficulty you arrive at the word *sale*, which represents the 5 of spades. If you wish to devise a word for the 3 of diamonds, it must begin with *d* because it is the diamond suit, and its final consonant must be *m* because the number 3 is represented by *m* in the Major System. Filling in with the first vowel, you arrive at the word *dam*, which is your Image Word for the 3 of diamonds.

Following is a list of the cards and their Memory Image Words. A few of the variations will be explained after you have had a chance to familiarise yourself with the list.

Clubs

CA—Cat
C2—Can
C3—Cameo
C4—Car
C5—Call
C6—Cash
C7—Cake
C8—Café
C9—Cab
C10—Case
CJ—Cadet
CQ—Cotton
CK—Club

Diamonds

DA—Day
D2—Dan
D3—Dam
D4—Dare
D5—Dale
D6—Dash
D7—Deck
D8—Daffy
D9—Dab
D10—Daze
DJ—Deadwood
DQ—Deaden
DK—Diamond

Hearts

HA—Hat
H2—Hen
H3—Ham
H4—Hair
H5—Hail
H6—Hash
H7—Hag
H8—Hoof
H9—Hub
H10—Haze
HJ—Headed
HQ—Heathen
HK—Heart

Spades

SA—Sat
S2—Sin
S3—Sum
S4—Sear
S5—Sale
S6—Sash
S7—Sack
S8—Safe
S9—Sap
S10—Seas
SJ—Sated
SQ—Satan
SK—Spade

In this system, aces count as 1, and the jacks and queens as 11 and 12, and 10 counts as 0, and the king simply as the name of the suit in which he resides. The Memory Words for the clubs and diamonds are in many cases the same as those for the Major System words for the seventies and teens, but this need not concern you, since the two lists will never come into conflict.

How does the memory expert dazzle his audience? The answer is quite simple: whenever a card is called out, he associates that card with the appropriate number of his Major System.

If, for example, the first card called out were the 7 of diamonds you would associate the word *deck* with the first word of your Major System, which is *day*. You might imagine the entire deck of a boat being bathed in daylight, making sure that in your association you smelled, saw, heard, tasted and touched as much as you could. If the next card called were the ace of hearts, you would associate the word of this card – *hat* – with the second word of your Major System: *Noah*. You might imagine Noah standing on the ark, wearing a gigantic rain-hat onto which the Flood is pouring and splashing in the most tremendous volume. You could actually imagine yourself as Noah, feeling the chill of the water and hearing the splashing, etc. If the next card called were the queen of spades, you would associate the word for that card – *Satan* – with your third Major System word: *Ma*. You might imagine your mother in a titanic struggle with Satan in the burning fires of hell, using as much motion, rhythm, colour and sensuality as possible. Throughout the memorisation of a pack of cards using the Major System as the pegs on which to hang the 52 items, you can see that you are clearly using both the logical, analytical, sequential and numerical left side of your brain, and the imaginative, colourful, rhythmical and sensual right side of your brain. From these few examples, I hope you can see how easy it can be to memorise an entire pack of cards in whatever order they happen to be presented to you. It is a most impressive feat to be able to perform in front of your friends.

Your facility for remembering cards can be taken a step further. It is possible to have someone randomly read you the names of all the cards in the pack, leaving out any six or seven. Without much hesitation, you can name these cards. There are two ways of doing this. The first is to use a technique similar to that explained in chapter 5. Whenever a card is called out, you associate the Image Word for that card within a larger concept, such as the block of ice previously mentioned. When all the cards have been presented, you simply run down the list of card Memory Words, noting those words that are not connected with the larger Memory Concept. If the 4 of clubs had been called, you might have pictured a car sliding across the huge cube of ice or being trapped within it. You could hardly forget this image, but if the 4 of clubs had not been called, you would immediately remember that you had nothing to remember.

The other system for this kind of feat is to mutate, or change, in some way the card Memory Image Word if that card is called. For example, if the king of clubs was called and your image for this was a caveman-like club, you could imagine the club being broken in half. Or if the card called was the 2 of hearts and your normal image of this was a simple farm hen, you might imagine it with an extraordinarily large tail.

The systems described in this chapter are basic to the remembering of cards, but it does not take much to see that in the actual playing of card games, a Memory System such as this can be of enormous help. You have probably watched people repeating over and over to themselves the cards that they know have been put down or which are in other players' hands, and you have probably seen them sigh with exasperation at their inability to remember accurately.

Onword

With your new Memory System, such tasks will become easy and a joy, and whether you use it for serious card playing or simply for enjoyment, throughout the process you will be exercising your creative memory powers and increasing the usefulness of your brain.

Raising your IQ through the Long Number Memory System

The long number memory test on page 23 will probably have been particularly difficult (most people, in IQ tests, cannot remember numbers more than 7 or 8 digits in length).

Given a long number such as 95862190377 to memorise, most people will try a variety of responses including: to repeat the build-up continually as the number is presented, eventually getting bogged down in the very repetition itself; to subdivide the number into two- or three-number groups, eventually losing both the order and content of these; to work out mathematical relationships between the numbers as they are presented, inevitably 'losing track'; or to 'picture' the number as it is presented, the picture becoming more and more blurred as the long number is presented.

If you think back to your own performance in the initial long number memory test, you will probably realise that your own approach was either one or a combination of those approaches just mentioned. Once again, the Major System comes to the rescue, making the task of memorising long numbers not only easy but enjoyable. Instead of using the Major System as a peg system for remembering lists of 100 or 1000, etc., you take advantage of its flexibility: going back to the basic code, and to the Basic Key Image Words you constructed for the numbers from 0 to 100, you use the Key Image Words in conjunction with the Link System to remember long numbers.

For example, take the number at the beginning of this chapter, 95862190377. It is composed, in sequence, of the following smaller numbers, each followed by its Major System Key Image Word:

95—Ball
86—Fish
21—Net
90—Base
37—Mac
7—Key

In order to remember this almost 'impossibly long' number, all you now have to do is to use the Basic Link System, making the words into a simple and imaginative little story. For example, you could imagine a brilliant, rainbow-coloured *ball* bouncing with a loud boing off the head of a gigantic and beautifully coloured *fish* that had just fought its way out of a very tangled and dripping-wet net, which was slowly collapsing to the *base* level of a pier, where it wrapped itself around a man, wearing a fawn-coloured and wind-blown *mac*, just as he was bending over to pick up the *key*, which had dropped onto the pier with a loud clang.

At the end of this paragraph close your eyes and re-envision the little story. Now, recalling the Key Image Words, transform them into the numbers, and you will get:

b—9
l—5
f—8
sh—6
n—2
t—1
b—9
s—0
m—3
c—7
k—7
95862190377

It is not essential to remember long numbers using only groups of two. It is just as easy, and sometimes even more easy, to consider the numbers in subgroups of three. Try this with the number 851429730584. It is composed of:

851—Fault
429—Rainbow

730—Cameos
584—Lever

In order to remember this number, which is even longer than the previous one, it is once again a matter of using your Basic Link System to make up a single little image story using your Basic Key Image Words. Using your right-brain imagination, you can imagine some gigantic universal force that could cause a break or a *fault* in beautiful and shimmering *rainbow*-coloured *cameos*, which were so heavy they needed a gigantic lever to move them. Once again, at the end of this paragraph, close your eyes and refilm the little image story on your inner screen. Now recall the words and, transforming them, you get:

f—8
l—5
t—1
r—4
n—2
b—9
c—7
m—3
s—0
l—5
v—8
r—4

851429730584

Another system for remembering long numbers, especially if you have not committed the Major System's Key Image Words to memory, is to improvise with the basic Major System Memory Code, making up 4-consonant words from the number you have to remember. For example, with a 16-digit number, such as 1582907191447620, you could make up the following 4-digit numbers and Key Image Words: 1582 – *telephone*, 9071 – *basket*, 9144 – *botherer*, 7620 – *cushions*.

Here you could imagine a loudly and melodically ringing red *telephone* being thrown in a long and graceful parabolic curve into a *basket*, where an annoying person (a *botherer*) is jammed bottom-down (as in comedy films), while other people are throwing multicoloured and multimaterialed *cushions* at him. Again, at the end of this paragraph close your eyes and imagine the story, then fill in the words and the numbers in the space opposite.

If you ever run into difficulty with the order of the words, you can resolve this simply by using, instead of the Link System, either the Number-Shape or the Number-Rhyme System. For example, using the original number at the beginning of this chapter, 95862190377, you would simply link *ball* to your Key Image for the number 1; *fish* to your Key Image for the number 2; net to your Key Image for the number 3; and so on.

You could also use both the Roman Room System and the Alphabet System, simply placing the words you had decoded from the long number either alphabetically or in your Roman Room. Decide which approach to the memorisation of long numbers is best for you. Then, to check on the amazing difference this method of number memorisation can make, go back to the original tests in chapter 2, and see just how easy those initial numbers were.

Onword

Once you have mastered this skill, you will have not only improved your memory and your creative imagination even further, but will have **actually raised your IQ**. One subsection of Intelligence Quotient measurements involves the ability to remember numbers. Between 6 and 7 is the average person's limit; a score of 9 or more puts you, in that subsection of the test, in the IQ range of 150 and more.

Telephone Number Memory System 16

Remembering telephone numbers turns out to be easier than forgetting, and once again it is the Major System that comes to the rescue in this situation.

Rather than being lodged in memory, most telephone numbers find themselves on scraps of paper in a limitless range of sizes, colours and shapes, in pockets, drawers, briefcases, and that general storehouse of frustration I call 'The Forgettory'. The procedure for remembering telephone numbers is to translate each digit of the number you have to remember into a letter from the basic code of the Major System. Using the letters you have transcribed, you make up catchy words and phrases that 'link you back' to both the number and the person.

For example, start with the ten people whose numbers you tried to remember in the initial test on page 23.

Telephone Numbers

Your health-food shop	787-5953
Your tennis partner	640-7336
Your local weather bureau	691-0262
Your local newsagent	242-9111
Your local florist	725-8397
Your local garage	781-3702
Your local theatre	869-9521
Your local nightclub	644-1616

| Your local community centre | 457-8910 |
| Your favourite restaurant | 354-6350 |

The following examples are possible solutions to these ten telephone numbers.

Your local health-food shop: 787-5953. This translates into the letters *g f g-l b l m*. Your memory phrase, starting with each number's letters, could be: *Good Food Guides: heaLthy Body heaLthy Mind*. In your imagination you would visualise healthy owners of the shop, and the Greek ideal of *mens sana in corpore sano*, perhaps even visualising Olympic Games in which all the participants had bought their food from this health-food shop.

Your tennis partner: 640-7336. This translates into the letters *sh r s-c m m sh*. Your visual memory phrase here might be: *SHows Real Skill – Can Make Masterly SHots*. Again you should visualise your tennis partner making the statement come true.

Your local weather bureau: 691-0262. This translates to the letters: *sh p d-s n sh n*. Here, if you can imagine yourself as a sculptor of the sun, making it into various shapes, and therefore yourself as god of meteorology, you can use a very condensed phrase that includes only the letters that translate back into the number: *SHaPeD SuNSHiNe!*

Your local newsagent: 242-9111. This translates to the letters *n r n-p d t d*. Again, you can use the condensing technique, imagining your local newsagent shouting: *'News! Read News! – uPDaTeD!'*

Your local florist: 725-8397. This translates to the letters *g n l-f m b g*. Imagine yourself just having given a bouquet of beautiful flowers to the one you love and wanting to shout about it to the world: *'Good News Lovers! Flowers Make Beautiful Gifts!'*

Your local garage: 781-3702. This translates into the letters *c f t-m g s n*. Imagine your garage as super-efficient, turning around every car within a day and giving it back to its owner in a condition as perfect as when it came off the assembly line: *Cars Fixed Today! Made Good aS New*.

Your local theatre: 869-9521. This translates to the letters *f sh p-p l n t*. Imagine that your local theatre is putting on a number of plays by Shakespeare and that as you attend each of the plays you experience the entire gamut of emotion: *Finest SHakespearian Productions Produce Laughter aNd Tears*.

Your local nightclub: 644-1616. This translates to the letters *ch r r-d j d j*. The latter part needs no changing, so all you have to do in this particular number is to find a little phrase for the first three letters, which is conveniently: *CHanges Revolving Records – DJ! DJ!*

Your local community centre: 457–8910. This translates to the letters *r I c-f b d s*. Imagine the whole joint jumping: *Really Lively Community – Football! Badminton! Dances! Swimming!*

Your favourite restaurant: 354–6350. This translates to the letters *m l r-ch m l s*. Imagine your restaurant offering excellent cuisine at reasonable prices: *My Lovely Restaurant – CHarges Moderate; Luscious Selections.*

The examples given above are, of course, very particular, and it will now be up to you to apply the system outlined to the telephone numbers that are important for you to remember. In some cases, the combination of numbers may present a greater than usual difficulty, and appropriate phrases or words may be almost impossible to devise. In such cases, the solutions are still fairly simple. In the first case, you may make up inappropriate words out of the numbers you have to deal with, and then use the basic system, making absurd and exaggerated images to link with the person whose telephone number you are trying to remember. For example, if the telephone number of one of your friends whose hobby is golf is 491-4276, you would take the Major System Memory Words for 49 (*rap*), 142 (*drain*) and 76 (cage). Your image for remembering this number would be of your friend rapping loudly on the drain, which has bars like a cage, with his golf club.

Now that you have mastered the basics of the Telephone Number Memory System, it is essential that you associate and link it to your own life. Therefore, in the space provided, make a note of the names and telephone numbers of at least ten people or places you need to remember, and before reading the next chapter make sure you have your own ten numbers firmly pictured in your memory. As you form the images, remember the Memory Principles, realising that the more enjoyable, humorous and imaginative you make the exercise, the better your memory for those numbers will be.

My Ten Most Important Telephone Numbers

1 _____
_____

2 _____
_____

3 _____
_____

4 _____
_____

5 _____
_____

6 _____
_____

7 _____
_____

8 _____
_____

9 _____
_____

10 _____
_____

Memory System for Schedules and Appointments

In this chapter two systems are introduced, the first of which is for immediate daily use, the second for remembering schedules and appointments for an entire week.

As with telephone numbers, many people find appointments and schedules hard to remember. They use similar systems for coping with their problem, the most common, of course, being the daily appointment book. Unfortunately, many people don't always keep their appointment books with them.

The first Memory System involves your basic Peg Systems. Simply equate the number in your system with the hour of your appointment. Since there are 24 hours in a day, you can either join shorter systems together, with an appropriate total of 24, or use the first 24 Peg Words in one of the larger systems.

Assume that you have the following appointments:

> 7– Early-morning group athletics practice
> 10– Dentist
> 1– Luncheon
> 6– Board meeting
> 10– Late film

At the beginning of the day, you run through the list and check for words with associations.

The time for your early-morning group athletics practice is 7.00 a.m., represented by the Major System Memory Word *key*. Imagine your entire team physically unlocking the door to super health with a big key.

At 10.00 a.m. (*daze*) you have an appointment with the dentist. Imagine him putting earphones on your head that play such soothing music that you are literally in a *daze*, unable to feel any pain. (What may be interesting in this example is the fact that if you imagine this particular situation, you may actually be able to reduce the pain!)

Your next appointment, at 1.00 p.m. (1300 hours), is for lunch. The Key Word here is *dam*. Imagine your luncheon table and luncheon guests, including yourself, sitting down for lunch at the top of an enormous *dam*, looking at the limpid lake on one side and the roaring waterfall on the other.

At 6.00 p.m. you have a board meeting. The Major System Memory Word for 18 (1800 hours) is *Daffy*. The association here is not difficult: imagine the confidential matters of your board meeting being discussed with Daffy Duck presiding.

Finally, you have an appointment at 10.00 p.m. (2200 hours) to see a late film. The Major System Memory Word is *nan*, so you can imagine going to the film with your grandmother, or if you like Indian food, imagine yourself eating the Indian bread (*nan*) throughout the film.

You can easily 'order' these five appointments, either by using the Link System to link the images you have just made or by simply placing each of the five images on your basic Number-Shape or Number-Rhyme System.

The second system for remembering schedules and appointments may be used for an entire week. Take Sunday as day 1 of the week and ascribe a number to each of the other days:

Sunday	1
Monday	2
Tuesday	3
Wednesday	4
Thursday	5
Friday	6
Saturday	7

Having given a number to the day, you treat the hours as they are treated in the first system discussed above, and as they appear in railway, shipping and airline timetables. The day is considered to have 24 hours, from 2400 (midnight) through 1.00 a.m. (0100), noon (1200), 1.00 p.m. (1300), and back to midnight (2400).

Thus, for any hour and day of the week a 2- or 3-digit number is formed – day first, hour second. All that is necessary is to translate the number into the word of a Major System list. Having arrived at the word, you link it with the appropriate appointment. For example, suppose you had an appointment to see a car you wanted to buy at 9.00 a.m. on Tuesday. Tuesday is represented by the number 3, which in the Major System translates to the letter *m*. The hour, 9, translates to the letters *b*, *p*. Referring to the basic list, you will see that the Key Word for Tuesday at 9.00 a.m. is *map*. To remember this appointment, you might imagine the car you are going to see as bursting through a giant map, wrapped in a giant map or driving across a giant map.

As another example, suppose you have an appointment for a guitar lesson at 5.00 p.m. (hour number 17) on a Thursday (day number 5). The number derived from Thursday at 5.00 p.m. is 517, the word for this being *leading*. To remember this, imagine yourself leading an entire orchestra with your solo guitar. Use the SMASHIN' SCOPE Memory Principles and imagine you can hear all the sounds, feel your guitar, see the audience, etc.

You may think this system a bit cumbersome because it requires a fairly thorough knowledge of the larger numbers in the Major System, but this can be overcome by 'rotating' the hours of the day to suit the times when you have most appointments. If your day does not usually start until 10.00 a.m., then 10.00 a.m. can be considered number 1 in your appointment memory system. In this manner, the most important and often-used hours in your day will nearly always be represented by only 2-digit numbers, i.e., the numbers from 10 to 100 in the Major System. As with the daily schedule memory technique, you can 'order' your week's schedules by attaching the images, in order, to the Major System.

Onword

For practical purposes, it is usually best to start on the Daily Memory System first, becoming skilled and familiar with it, and then move on to the Weekly Memory System.

Memory System for Dates in the Twentieth Century

When you have finished this chapter you will be able to give the correct day of the week for any date between the years 1900 and 2000!

Two systems may be used, the first of which is faster and simpler and applies to only one given year, whereas the second spans 100 years and is a little more difficult. These systems owe much to Harry Lorayne, a well-known North American memory expert. Using the first of these systems, assume that you wish to know the day for any given date in the year 1971. In order to accomplish what may sound like a rather considerable feat, all that is necessary is to remember the following number:

377426415375

'Impossible!' you might say, but once this system is explained you will see that it is in fact very clear and easy to operate. The individual digits of the 12-digit number represent the first Sunday for each month of the year 1971. The first Sunday in April, for example, falls on the fourth day of the month, the first Sunday in December falls on the fifth day of the month, and so on. Once you have remembered this number (if you have difficulty, refer back to the chapter on Long Number Memory) you will be able rapidly to calculate the day of the week for any date in the year.

It is best to explain this concept with examples, so let us assume that your birthday fell on 28 April, and that you wished to know what day the date represented. Taking the fourth digit from your Memory Number you would see that the first Sunday fell on the

4th. By the process of adding sevens to this initial Sunday date you rapidly calculate that the second Sunday of the month fell on the 11th (4 + 7 = 11); the third Sunday of the month fell on the 18th and the fourth Sunday fell on the 25th. Knowing this, you recite the remaining dates and the days of the week until you arrive at the date in question: 26 April = Monday; 27 April = Tuesday; 28 April = Wednesday. So your birthday fell on a Wednesday in 1971.

Suppose you wish to know the final day of the year. The process is similar. Knowing that the first Sunday of the last month falls on the 5th day, you add the three sevens representing the following Sundays to arrive at Sunday 26th. Reciting the next few dates and days we get: 27th Monday; 28th Tuesday; 29th Wednesday; 30th Thursday; 31st (the last day of the year) – a Friday.

As you can see, this system can be applied to any year for which you may especially need to know the days for dates. All you have to do is to make up a Memory Number for the first Sunday or, for that matter, the first Monday, Tuesday, etc., of each month of the year; add sevens where appropriate to bring you near to the day in question; and recite to that day.

An interesting tip in making use of the Memory Number of one year with relation to surrounding years is that with each year the first date for the days at the beginning of the month goes down one, with the exception of leap years, when the extra day produces a jump of two for the following year. In the years 1969, 1970, 1971, for instance, the first Sunday for January fell respectively on the 5th, 4th and 3rd days of the month.

The second of the two systems to be introduced in this chapter is for calculating the day for any date from 1900 to 2000. It is necessary in this system to ascribe to each month a number that will always remain the same. The numbers for the months are as follows:

January	1	July	0
February	4	August	3
March	4	September	6
April	0	October	1
May	2	November	4
June	5	December	6

Some people suggest that these be remembered using associations such as January is the first month, the fourth letter in February is *r*, which represents 4, and so on, but I think that it is better to use the number:

144025036146

making the words *DRaweR*, *SNaiL*, *SMaSH* and *THRuSH*. These can then be linked by imagining a drawer on which a snail's shell is smashed by a thrush. In this way the key numbers for the months can be remembered.

In addition to the key numbers for the months, the years themselves have key numbers, and I have listed them, from 1900 to 2000.

0	1	2	3	4	5	6
1900	1901	1902	1903	1909	1904	1905
1906	1907	1913	1908	1915	1910	1911
1917	1912	1919	1914	1920	1921	1916
1923	1918	1924	1925	1926	1927	1922
1928	1929	1930	1931	1937	1932	1933
1934	1935	1941	1936	1943	1938	1939
1945	1940	1947	1942	1948	1949	1944
1951	1946	1952	1953	1954	1955	1950
1956	1957	1958	1959	1965	1960	1961
1962	1963	1969	1964	1971	1966	1967
1973	1968	1975	1970	1976	1977	1972
1979	1974	1980	1981	1982	1983	1978
1984	1985	1986	1987	1993	1988	1989
1990	1991	1997	1992	1999	1994	1995
	1996		1998			2000

This system is not so easy to master, but with a little practice it can become almost second nature. The method is as follows: given the month, numerical date and the year, you add the number represented by the month key to the number of the date, and add this total to the key number representing the year in question. From the total you subtract all the sevens, and the remaining number represents the day in the week, taking Sunday as day 1. If the total is exactly divisible by 7, e.g. 28, subtract one less 7 (in this case 3 × 7 = 21 instead of 4 × 7 = 28).

In order to check this system, we will take a couple of examples. The day we will try to hunt down is 19 March 1969. Our key number for March is 4, which we must then add to the date in question, which is 19: 19 + 4 = 23. To this total we must add the key number for the year 1969. Referring to the list we find that this is 2. Adding 2 to our previous total we arrive at $23 + 2 = 25$. Subtracting all the sevens from this ($3 \times 7 = 21$) we arrive at $25 - 21 = 4$. The day in question is consequently the 4th day of the week, which is a Wednesday. The second date is 23 August 1972. Our key number for August is 3, which we add to 23, giving 26. The key number for the year 1972 is 6, which added to 26 gives us 32. Subtracting all the sevens ($4 \times 7 = 28$) from 32 we arrive at 4. The 4th day of the week is a Wednesday, which is the day for 23 August 1972.

The only exception to this rule occurs in leap years, and then only in the months of January and February. Your calculations will be identical, but for these two months the day of the week will be one day earlier than the day you calculate.

Onword

As with other systems, the best way to gain confidence with these two is to practise them. Start with the easier one, then graduate to the more advanced.

Memory System for Important Historical Dates

The two systems you have just learned enable you to remember the day for any date in the twentieth century. The next system will assist you in the memorisation of significant dates in history.

In chapter 2 one of the memory tests included a list of ten such dates. They were:

1 1666 Great Fire of London
2 1770 Beethoven's birthday
3 1215 Signing of Magna Carta
4 1917 Russian Revolution
5 1454 First printing press
6 1815 Battle of Waterloo
7 1608 Invention of the telescope
8 1905 Einstein's Theory of Relativity
9 1789 French Revolution
10 1776 American Declaration of Independence

The method for remembering these or any other such dates is simple; it is similar to the method for remembering telephone numbers. All you have to do is to make a word or string of words from the letters that represent the numbers of the date. In most cases, there is no point in including the 1 representing the thousand, since you know the approximate date in any case. Let us try this system on the dates above:

1   The Great Fire of London in 1666 practically destroyed the city, leaving it a heap of ashes. Our memory phrase for the date 1666 would thus be: *aSHes, aSHes, aSHes! or CHarred aSHes Generally.*

2   Beethoven is famous for many musical accomplishments, but perhaps his greatest achievement was the Ninth Symphony, in which he included a choir. His style of music made full use of the percussion instruments. Knowing this, remembering his birthday in 1770 becomes easy: *Crashing CHoral Symphony.*

3   The signing of the Magna Carta in 1215 marked a new age of sense and reason. To remember this date, we can use the phrase *New Document – Liberalisation.*

4   The Russian Revolution of 1917 was an uprising of the people against what they considered oppression. They demanded greater equality in the form of communism. Our Memory Phrase: *People Demand Communism.*

5   Printing presses are often great rotating machines that churn out thousands of pages a minute. We can imagine a small version of this as the first printing press, in 1454, which can be remembered by the word *RoLleR.*

6   The Battle of Waterloo in 1815 was a triumph for Wellington but can be considered fatal for Napoleon. Once again we use a Memory Word rather than a Memory Phrase to remember the date: *FaTaL.*

7   The invention of the telescope by Hans Lippershey in 1608 changed the way in which man saw the sky. Our Memory Phrase: *CHanged Sky Focus.*

8   In 1905 Einstein's Theory of Relativity shed new light on the way in which matter and energy exist. His theory solved a number of puzzles that had occupied man but also gave rise to many more. Our Key Word: *PuZZLe.*

9   In the French Revolution in 1789 the king was ranged against the people. Hence, we can remember the date by *King Fights People.*

10 The American Declaration of Independence in 1776 marked in America a feeling of optimism and confidence in a new way of life. This can be encapsulated in the one word: *CoCKSure.*

Remembering

Birthdays, Anniversaries, and Days and Months of Historical Dates

20

The next system will be easy for you because it makes use of systems you have already learned. It is also easier than most other systems suggested for remembering such items because the large Memory System you have learned – the Major System – may be used as a 'key' for the months and days (other systems usually require code names that have to be especially devised for the months).

The system works as follows: months are assigned the numbers 1 to 12 and given the appropriate Key Word from the Major System.

Month	Key Word
January	day
February	Noah
March	Ma
April	Ra
May	law
June	jaw
July	key
August	fee
September	bay
October	daze
November	Dad
December	Dan

To remember a birthday, anniversary or historical date, all that is necessary is to form a linked image between the month- and day-words and the date you wish to remember. For example, your girlfriend's birthday falls on 17th June. The Key Word from the Major System for June is *jaw*; and the Key Word for 17 is *deck*. Imagine your girlfriend spending a deliriously happy day with you on the *deck* of a large boat, and the big *jaws* seeing your state of bliss, grins from ear to ear!

You wish to remember your parents' wedding anniversary, which falls on 25 February. The Key Word for February is *Noah*; and the Key Word for 25 is *nail*. Imagine *Noah*, who 'married' the pairs of animals, trying to marry your parents by *nailing* them together!

Historical dates are just as easy to remember. For example, the date when the United Nations came into formal existence was 24 October. The Major System Key Word for October is *daze*; and the Key Word for 24 is *Nero*. Imagine a horse, *dazed* from the blaze caused by *Nero*'s burning city, running into a situation where there is no strife.

To help you further in remembering birthdays, anniversaries, and the days and months of historical dates, it is useful to use a diary system such as the Universal Personal Organiser (UPO). (See page 181.) This system makes use of all the Memory Principles, and has specific sections devoted to enabling you to use Memory Systems for the memorisation of items such as that discussed in this chapter.

There is one small problem in this system, and this is the possibility of *knowing* the date but forgetting to remember it! This can be overcome by making a habit of checking through, on a regular basis, your memory links for the coming week or two.

Onword

The Memory System outlined in this chapter can be linked effectively with the previous system for remembering historical dates by year. In this way, you will have provided yourself with a *complete* date remembering system.

Memory Systems for Vocabulary and Language

21

Preview

- The 100 Basic Words that Make Up 50 Per Cent of All Conversation

Vocabulary is the basic building block of language, so it is desirable and necessary to develop methods of learning and remembering words more easily.

As mentioned in my books *The Speed Reading Book* and *Master Your Memory*, vocabulary is considered to be the most important single factor not only in the development of efficient reading but also in academic and business success. This is not surprising when one realises that the size of one's vocabulary is usually an indication of the range of one's knowledge.

One of the better ways of remembering words is to learn the prefixes (letters, syllables or words recurring before root words), the suffixes (letters, syllables or words recurring at the end of root words) and the roots (words from which other words are derived) that occur most frequently in the language you are attempting to learn. A comprehensive list of these appears in the vocabulary chapters of *The Speed Reading Book*.

Here are some more tips on how to improve your word memory:

1 Browse through a good dictionary, studying the ways in which the prefixes, suffixes and roots of the language are used. Whenever possible, use association to strengthen your recall.

2 Introduce a fixed number of new words into your vocabulary every day. New words are retained only if the principle of repetition, as explained earlier, is practised. Use your new words in context and as many times as possible after you have initially learned them.

3 Consciously *look* for new words in the language. This directing of your attention, known as mental set, leaves the 'hooks' of your memory more open to catch new linguistic fish!

These are general learning aids to assist your memory in acquiring knowledge of a language. They may be applied to English, as a means of improving your present vocabulary, or to any foreign languages you are beginning to learn. Having established a *general* foundation for learning words, let us be more specific in the remembering of particular words. As with other memory systems, the key word is **association.** In the context of language learning, it is well to associate sounds, **images** and similarities, using the fact that certain languages are grouped in 'families' and have related words.

To give you an idea of this linking method, I shall consider a few words from English, French, Latin and German. In English, you want to remember the word *vertigo,* which means 'dizziness' or 'giddiness', and in which a person feels as if surrounding objects were turning around. To imprint this word on the memory you associate the sound of it with the phrase *where to go?* which is the kind of question you would ask if you felt that all surrounding objects were rotating about you.

Two words that many people confuse in the English language are *acrophobia,* which is a morbid fear of heights, and *agoraphobia,* a morbid fear of open spaces. The distinction can be firmly established if you associate the *acro* in *acrophobia* with *acrobat* (a person who performs at a great height) and the *agora* in *agoraphobia* with *agriculture,* bringing to mind images of open fields (though the Greek word *agora* actually means 'marketplace').

Foreign languages are more approachable when one realises that they form groups. Practically all European languages (with the exception of Finnish, Hungarian and Basque) are part of the Indo-European group, and consequently they contain a number of words similar in both sound and meaning. For example, the words for *father*: German, *Vater*; Latin, *pater*; French, *père*; Italian and Spanish, *padre*. A knowledge of Latin is of enormous help in understanding all the Romance languages, in which many of the words are similar. The Latin word for *love* is *amor*. Related to *love* in the English language is the word *amorous*, which means 'inclined to love; in love; and of, or pertaining to, love'. The links are obvious. Similarly, you have the Latin word for *God*: *Deus*. In English, the words deity and deify mean, respectively, 'divine status; a god; the Creator' and 'to make a god of'.

French was derived from the speech of the Roman legionnaires, who called the head *testa*, hence *tête*, and the arm *brachium*, hence *bras*, etc. About 50 per cent of ordinary English speech is derived from Latin (plus Greek) either directly or by way of Norman French, leading to many direct similarities between French and English.

In addition to similarities based on language grouping, foreign words can be remembered in a manner not unlike that explained for remembering English words. Since we are discussing French, the following two examples are appropriate: in French, the word for *book* is *livre*. This can be remembered more readily if you think of the first four letters of the word *library*, which is a place where books are classified and studied. The French word for *pen* is *plume*, which in English refers to a bird's feather, especially a large one used for ornament. This immediately brings to mind the quill pen used widely before the invention of the steel nib, fountain pen and ballpoint pen. The link-chain *plume – feather – quill – pen* will make remembering the French word a simple task.

Apart from Latin, Greek and French, the rest of English is largely Anglo-Saxon, going back to German, giving rise to countless words that are the same in German and English – *will, hand, arm, bank, halt, wolf*, etc., whereas others are closely related: *light (Licht), night (Nacht), book (Buch), stick (Stock), ship (Schiff)* and *house (Haus)*.

Learning languages, both our own and those of other people, need not be the frustrating and depressing experience it so often is. It is simply a matter of organising the information you want to learn in such a way as to enable your memory to 'hook on' to every available scrap of information.

Brain Bites

One way to get a head start in learning is to realise that in most languages, 50 per cent of all conversation is made up of only 100 words. If you apply the Major System to the memorisation of these you are already 50 per cent of the way toward being able to understand the basic conversation of any native speaker.

For your convenience, the 100 basic words in the English language are listed below. You will find that if you compare them with their counterparts in, say, French, German, Swedish, Italian, Spanish, Portuguese, Russian, Chinese, Japanese and Esperanto, nearly 50 per cent of these are almost the same as in English, with only minor variations in the accent and accentuation of the words. These translations are provided for you in *Master Your Memory*.

The 100 Basic Words that Make Up 50 Per Cent of All Conversation

1	a, an	21	to go (I go)	40	many
2	after	22	good	41	me
3	again	23	goodbye	42	more
4	all	24	happy	43	most
5	almost	25	have (I have)	44	much
6	also	26	he	45	my
7	always	27	hello	46	new
8	and	28	here	47	no
9	because	29	how	48	not
10	before	30	I	49	now
11	big	31	I am	50	of
12	but	32	if	51	often
13	can (I can)	33	in	52	on
14	come (I come)	34	know (I know)	53	one
15	either/or	35	last	54	only
16	find (I find)	36	like (I like)	55	or
17	first	37	little	56	other
18	for	38	love (I love)	57	our
19	friend	39	make (I make)	58	out
20	from			59	over
				60	people

61	place	75	their	87	us
62	please	76	them	88	use (I use)
63	same	77	then	89	very
64	see (I see)	78	there is,	90	we
65	she		there are	91	what
66	so	79	they	92	when
67	some	80	thing	93	where
68	sometimes	81	think (I	94	which
69	still		think)	95	who
70	such	82	this	96	why
71	tell (I tell)	83	time	97	with
72	thank you	84	to	98	yes
73	that	85	under	99	you
74	the	86	up	100	your

Applying the Memory Principles to the memorisation of these words and others, you will find that language learning can be the easy, enjoyable task that most children find it to be. Adults can learn languages as well as children. Children simply open their minds more to the language and are not afraid to make mistakes. They repeat and make associations with the basics, listen more attentively, copy and mimic, and generally have a thoroughly good time without as much instruction as we adults think we need.

Part Three

Mind Maps®

for Memory

Mind Maps®:
Notes for
Remembering

22

Most people forget what they note because they use only a tiny fraction of their brain in the note-taking process. The Mind-Mapping technique will allow you to remember a whole book!

Standard note-taking systems use sentences, phrases, lists and lines, and numbers. Such systems use only the left-cortex Memory Principles of words, lists, logic, order, sequence and number, leaving out imagination, association, exaggeration, contraction, absurdity, humour, colour, rhythm, the senses, sexuality and sensuality.

In order to make notes well, you have to break with tradition and use both the left and right sides of your cortex, as well as all the fundamental Memory Principles. In this system of note-taking, you use blank unlined pages, using a Key Memory Image (right brain) that summarises the central theme of the note you are making. From this central image you have a series of connecting lines (left cortex) on which are written (left cortex) or drawn (right cortex) the Key Image Words or actual images themselves of the main sub-areas and sub-themes you wish to note. Connected to these lines are more lines, again on which you place Key Image Words or Key Images themselves. In this way you build up a multidimensional, associative, imaginative and colourful **Mind Map** Memory Note of everything you wish to note.

Noting in this way, you will not only remember almost immediately and totally everything you write down because of the application of all the Memory Principles to this new multidimensional mnemonic note-taking approach but you will also find that the approach allows you to understand, analyse and think critically about whatever it is you are noting, while at the same time it gives you more time to pay attention to either the lecturer or the book from which you are learning. This technique and its applications are more fully outlined in my books *The Mind Map Book* and *Use Your Head*.

As an example, one of the editors responsible for revising this book used the **Mind Map** shown on Colour Plate III as a way of re-organising and summarising all the information contained in these chapters. A natural aggregation appeared: general information; specific systems; the Major Memory System and its application, and **Mind Maps** and their application.

Using Key Words and Key Images the **Mind Mapping** technique enables you to remember an entire book in one clear, single-sided, pictorial representation. The Memory and Creative Thinking Principles thus applied in your **Mind Map** notes enable you to tackle any new subject with ease and pass tests with 'flying colours'.

Onword

The following chapters show how to apply the Mind Map to the much-requested area of remembering which name goes with which face; recalling the 'forgotten' item/place/number; remembering for examinations; memorising for speeches, jokes, poems and books; and catching those elusive dreams.

Remembering Names and Faces

23

Remembering names and faces is one of the most important aspects of our lives, and one of the most difficult.

The reason for the difficulty lies in the fact that in most instances the names have no real 'connection' to the faces. In earlier ages it was exactly the opposite, and the whole system developed for giving people names was based on memory and association: the man you regularly saw covered in white flour with dough all over his hands was Mr Baker; the man you regularly saw in his own and everyone else's garden was Mr Gardener; the man who laboured all day over a hot fire pounding metal was Mr Blacksmith, and so on. As the generations changed and the family name became more and more removed from its original meaning, the task of the memorisation of names and faces became increasingly difficult, reaching the current situation in which the name is a word with no immediate associations with the face.

There are two major methods of coping with this situation, each method supporting the other. The first is the Buzan Social Etiquette Method; the second, the Mnemonic Method.

The Buzan Social Etiquette Method for Remembering Names and Faces

The Buzan Social Etiquette Method for remembering names and faces guarantees that you will never again find yourself in a situation where you are introduced rapidly to five people and hurriedly repeat, 'Pleased to meet you, pleased to meet you, pleased to meet you, pleased to meet you, pleased to meet you,' having been introduced only to the five pairs of shoes at which you look in embarrassment because you know you are immediately going to forget all the names anyway (which you do!).

The Social Etiquette Method requires just two simple things of you:

1 an **interest** in the people you meet
2 **politeness**

The method is the same as one that you might find described in a book of etiquette, yet even writers of etiquette books often fail to realise that the original rules were made not simply to enforce rigid disciplines but to allow people to interact on a friendly basis, the rules being structured formally only in order to enable the people to meet and *remember* one another.

Select from the following Social Etiquette Memory Steps those that will most help you.

The Social Etiquette Memory Steps
1 • Mental Set

Before you enter a situation in which you will meet people, mentally prepare yourself to succeed. Many people enter such situations 'knowing' that they have a bad memory for names and faces and consequently set about proving it to themselves. If you 'know' that your memory is going to improve, you will notice immediate improvement. When preparing yourself for meeting people, try to make sure that you are as poised and relaxed as possible and, also, that wherever possible you have given yourself a two- to five-minute break for preparation.

2 ● Observe

When you are meeting people, make sure you look them straight in the eye. Don't shuffle around, with your eyes on the floor or looking into the distance. As you look at someone's face, be aware of the special facial characteristics, for this will help you also in the second mnemonic approach to the memorisation of names and faces. On pages 152 to 154 there is a 'guided tour' from the top of the head to the tip of the chin, enumerating the various characteristics and the ways in which they can be classified and typified. The more you become skilled at the art of observation, the more you will realise just how different one face is from another.

If you can sharpen your observational powers, you will have made a giant step toward the improvement of your memory. Blank looking, instead of real seeing, is one of the major causes for poor memory.

You can prepare your mind for this by 'exercising' your observational powers in public places. At different times give yourself different parts of the face to look at, so that on one day you might concentrate on noses, another day on eyebrows, another day on ears, another on general head shapes, etc. You will find to your surprise that each part of each face varies enormously from person to person, and that your increasing observation of the differences will help you to remember the new faces that you meet.

3 ● Listen

Consciously *listen*, paying attention as much as you possibly can to the sound of the name of the person to whom you are being introduced. This is a crucial stage of the introductory process, at which point many people fail because they were concentrating more on the fact that they were going to forget than on the sound of the name of the person to whom they were being introduced.

4 ● Request Repetition

Even if you have heard the name fairly well, politely say something in the order of 'I'm sorry, would you mind repeating the name?' Repetition is an important memory aid; each repetition of any item you wish to learn greatly increases the probability of your remembering it.

5 ● Verify the Pronunciation

Once you have been given the name, immediately confirm, by asking the person to whom the name belongs, if you have the correct pronunciation. This confirms your interest and once again repeats the name, increasing the probability of your remembering it.

6 • Request the Spelling
If there is any doubt about the spelling of the name, politely or playfully ask for the spelling, again confirming your interest and allowing another natural repetition of the name.

7 • Your New Hobby – Derivations
With a natural enthusiasm, explain that one of your new hobbies is the background and derivation of names, and politely ask the person to whom you have been introduced if he or she knows anything about the history of his or her own family name. (Be sure you know the history of your own surname!) It may surprise you to know that on average 50 per cent of people not only know at least some part of the background of their families' nomenclature but most of them are enthusiastic about discussing it. Once again you will have confirmed your interest in the individual, as well as having laid the ground for more repetition.

8 • Exchange Cards
The Japanese have developed card-exchange as a major social function, realising how useful it is for memory. If you are really interested in remembering people's names, make sure you have a very presentable card to give them, and in most cases they will give you their own or write the details down for you.

9 • Repetition in Conversation
Carrying the principles of interest, politeness and repetition further, make sure that during conversations with people newly met you repeat their names wherever possible. This repetition helps to implant the name more firmly in your memory, and it is also socially more rewarding, for it involves the other person more intimately in the conversation. It is far more satisfying for them to hear you say, 'Yes, as Mary has just said . . .' than to hear you say, 'Yes, as she [as you point] has just said . . .'

10 • Repeat Internally
During any little pause in the conversation look analytically and with interest at the various people who are speaking and about

whom others are speaking, repeating internally to yourself the names that by now will be becoming second nature to you.

11 ● Check During Longer Breaks
If you have gone to get a drink for someone or for yourself, or for any other reason are momentarily alone in a crowd, spend the time scanning everyone you have met, repeating to yourself their names, the spelling of their names, any background material you have gathered about the names, plus any other items of interest that have arisen during the conversation. In this way, you will be surrounding each name with associations, thus building up a mapped network in your own mind that will increase the probability of future recall. You will be positively using the process described in chapter 24, on re-remembering.

12 ● Repetition at Parting
As you say farewell, make sure you use the name of the person to whom you are saying it. Thus, by this time you will have used both the primacy and recency time-aspects of memory as outlined in chapter 11, having consolidated both your initial and final moments during the 'learning period'.

13 ● Reviews
a *Mental.* When you have parted from the new people, quickly flash through your mind all the names and faces of those you have just met.

b *Photographs.* When possible (for example, at a party), get photographs (either the formal ones or informal ones) of the event.

c *Your names and faces memory diary.* If you are interested in becoming a real Master Memoriser of names, keep a special diary in which you quickly sketch and make a Mind Map (see chapter 22) of the faces of those you have met, the names that attach to them plus any other Key Image Word information. A diary system such as the Universal Personal Organiser (UPO) is useful for this exercise.

d *Personal card file.* Keep a card file, noting on each card the time, place and date at which you met the person concerned. Keeping these cards in Mind Map form, especially using image and colour, increases the value enormously.

e *Mind Mapping.* Keep a general Mind Map recording
your specific successes, and the Memory Foundations
and Principles that worked particularly well for you.
Use a mental Mind Map as you progress.

14 ● The Reversal Principle

Wherever possible, reverse the processes through which you
have just been. For example, when being introduced, repeat your
own name, give the spelling, and if it seems appropriate even
give the background. Similarly, make sure you present, where
appropriate, your personal card. Throughout conversations, if
you are referring to yourself, use your own name. This will help
others to remember you, as well as encouraging them to use their
names rather than pronouns. In addition to being more polite,
this approach will make the entire conversation more personal,
enjoyable and friendly.

15 ● Pace Yourself

There is a tendency, because of the stress of the initial meeting
situation, to rush through it. The great names-and-faces memorisers
and founders of social etiquette invariably take their time, making
sure they have said at least one personal thing to everyone they
meet. The Queen of England is a good example.

16 ● Have Fun

If you make the learning of names and faces a serious and *enjoyable*
game, the right side of your brain will feel far more free and open
to make the imaginative associations and connections necessary
for good memory. Children have 'better memories' for names and
faces than adults *not* because their minds are superior but simply
because they naturally apply all the principles outlined in this book.

17 ● The Plus-one Principle

If you would normally remember only between two to five of
30 people you have newly met, as the average person would, give
yourself the goal of *one more* than you would normally remember.
This establishes in your mind the principle of success and does not
place the unnecessary stress of your trying to be perfect first time
out. Apply the Plus-one Principle each time you are in a new
Situation and your road to success in the memorisation of names
and faces is guaranteed.

A useful exercise/game at this stage is to take the first letter of each of the 17 Social Etiquette Memory Steps, and to make a memorable acronym of that. Use all the SMASHIN' SCOPE Principles!

The Mnemonic Names and Faces Memory Principles

The Mnemonic Principles for remembering names and faces are identical to those outlined in chapter 4, emphasising: (1) imagination, and (2) association. The steps are as follows:

1 Make sure you have a clear mental image of the person's name.
2 Make sure you can actually 'hear again' the sound of the person's name.
3 Very carefully examine the face of the person to whom you are being introduced, noting in detail the characteristics outlined on pages 152 to 154.
4 Look for facial characteristics that are unusual, extraordinary or unique.
5 Mentally reconstruct the person's face, using your imagination in the way that a cartoonist does to exaggerate any noteworthy features.
6 Associate, using your imagination, exaggeration and the general Memory Principles, any of the outstanding features with the name of the person.

The quickest and easiest way for you to learn the application of these principles is to put them immediately into practice. On pages 155 to 158, I have doubled the number of faces and names you were asked to remember in the original test on pages 24 to 26. I have given suggestions on how you might apply the principles to remembering the names associated with five of the faces. Look carefully at them and at the remaining 15, remembering as many as you can, then test yourself at the end of the chapter.

Memorisation of Faces

If you wanted, for example, to remember the names of the faces on pages 155 to 158, you would simply apply the techniques outlined looking closely at the faces, finding some characteristics that you could imaginatively associate with the name, and then making your mnemonic image.

For example, *Mr Mapley* (No. 9) is easy to remember in that his face is deeply furrowed and lined, and that his hair is similarly laced with patterns – thus a map, leading to Mapley.

Mr Suzuki (No. 12) has particularly pronounced eyebrows, which you could imagine as the flamboyant handlebars of a Suzuki motorbike.

Ms Knight (No. 15) has hair that hangs – thus you might imagine her bending her head down from the top of a castle, with some valiant knight climbing up her tresses to rescue her.

Mr Burn (No.19) has very close-cropped and dark hair. You might imagine that his face was a countryside and that his hair was the result of a gigantic bush or forest fire that had *burned* all the vegetation.

Ms Hammond (No. 20), although she looks like the typical 'blonde beauty', also has a jowl structure that could remind you of the best leg of pork – ham!

One other point about remembering people: if you are *certain* that you will be meeting a person only once and are not concerned with your long-term memory of the name and the face, it is often useful to use an outstanding item of clothing that the person might be wearing. This method, of course, is no good for long-term memory, since a person will probably not be wearing the same clothes next time. The same point applies to hairstyles and beards.

Now check your memory of the faces and names you have linked and fill in the names at the end of the chapter.

Head and Facial Characteristics
1 • Head

You will usually first meet a person face-to-face, so before dealing with the rundown of separate characteristics, we will consider the head as a whole. Look for the general shape of the entire bone structure. You will find that this can be: a) large; b) medium; or c) small. And that within these three categories the following shapes can be found: a) square; b) rectangular; c) round; d) oval; e) triangular, with the base at the chin and the point at the scalp; f) triangular, with the base at the scalp and the point at the chin, g) broad; h) narrow; i) big-boned; or j) fine-boned.

Fairly early in your meeting, you may see the head from the side and will be surprised at how many different shapes heads seen from this view can take: a) square; b) rectangular; c) oval; d) broad; e) narrow; f) round; g) flat at the front; h) flat on top; i) flat at the back; j) domed at the back; k) face angled with jutting chin and

slanted forehead; or l) face angled with receding chin and prominent forehead.

2 ● Hair
In earlier days, when hairstyles used to be more consistent and
lasting, hair served as a better memory hook than it does now. The
advent of dyes, sprays, wigs and almost infinitely varied styles
makes identification by this feature a tricky business. Some of the
more basic characteristics, however, can be listed as follows:

Men: a) thick; b) fine; c) wavy; d) straight; e) parted; f) receding;
g) bald; h) cropped; i) medium; j) long; k) frizzy; and l) colour
(only in notable cases).

Women: a) thick; b) thin; or c) fine. Because of the variability
in women's hairstyles it is not advisable to try to remember them
from this characteristic.

3 ● Forehead
Foreheads can generally be divided into the following categories:
a) high; b) wide; c) narrow between hairline and eyebrows;
d) narrow between temple and temple; e) smooth; f) lined
horizontally; or g) lined vertically.

4 ● Eyebrows
a) thick; b) thin; c) long; d) short; e) meeting at the middle; f) spaced
apart; g) flat; h) arched; i) winged; j) bushy; or k) tapered.

5 ● Eyelashes
a) thick; b) thin; c) long; d) short; e) curled; or f) straight.

6 ● Eyes
a) large; b) small; c) protruding; d) deep-set; e) close together;
f) spaced apart; g) slanted outward; h) slanted inward; i) coloured;
j) iris – entire circle seen; or k) iris – circle covered partly by upper
and/or lower lid. Attention may also be paid in some cases to the
lid above and the bag below the eye, both of which can be large
or small, smooth or wrinkled, puffy or firm.

7 ● Nose
When seen from the front: a) large; b) small; c) narrow;
d) medium; e) wide; or f) crooked. When seen from the side:
a) straight; b) flat; c) pointed; d) blunt; e) snub or upturned;
f) Roman or aquiline; g) Greek, forming straight line with

forehead; or h) concave (caved in). The base of the nose can also vary considerably in relation to the nostrils: a) lower; b) level; or c) a little higher. The nostrils themselves can also vary: a) straight; b) curved down; c) flaring; d) wide; e) narrow; or f) hairy.

8 ● Cheekbones
Cheekbones are often linked very closely with the characteristics of the face when seen front-on, but the following three characteristics are often worth noting: a) high; b) prominent; or c) obscured.

9 ● Ears
Ears are a part of the face that few people pay attention to, and yet their individuality can be greater than any other feature. They may be: a) large; b) small; c) gnarled; d) smooth; e) round; f) oblong; g) triangular; h) flat against the head; i) protruding; j) hairy; k) large lobed; l) no lobe; or m) uneven. This feature is of course more appropriate as a memory hook with men than with women, because the latter often cover their ears with hair.

10 ● Lips
a) long upper lip; b) short upper lip; c) small; d) thick (bee-stung); e) wide; f) thin; g) upturned; h) downturned; i) Cupid's bow; j) well-shaped; or k) ill-defined.

11 ● Chin
When seen straight-on, the chin may be: a) long; b) short; c) pointed; d) square; e) round; f) double (or multiple); g) cleft; or h) dimpled. When seen from the side, it will be: a) jutting; b) straight; c) double (or multiple); or d) receding.

12 ● Skin
a) smooth; b) rough; c) dark; d) fair; e) blemished or marked in some way; f) oily; g) dry; h) blotchy; i) doughy; j) wrinkled; k) furrowed; l) coloured or sun-tanned; or m) freckled.

Other characteristics of faces, especially men's, include the various and varied growth of facial hair ranging from short sideburns to the full-blooded and face-concealing beard with moustache. There is no point in listing all the variations. It should suffice to note that these hirsute phenomena do exist, but that they, like hairstyles and colours, can change overnight.

1 Mr Mogambi

2 Mr Knorr

3 Ms Woodrowe

4 Mr Kokowski

5 Mrs Volkein

6 Mr Cliffe

7 Mr Momatt

8 Miss Ashton

9 Mr Mapley

10 Mr Dewhurst

11 Ms Jabanardi

12 Mr Suzuki

13 Mr Welsh

14 Mr Macinnes

15 Ms Knight

16 Ms Parsons

17 Ms Cook

18 Mr Pong

19 Mr Burn

20 Ms Hammond

As you establish your Social Etiquette and Mnemonic Memory techniques for names and faces, it is useful to have a Basic Image List of names you are likely to meet. In your Basic Image List simply have a standard image for common names that you can immediately link to the outstanding facial characteristic of anyone who has that name. Following is a list of examples that you can expand to fit your own social context:

Ashcroft the smouldering roof of a burned-out farm building with masses of flaky grey ash

Blake a gigantic, limpid blue lake in the shape of the letter B

Chalk the white cliffs of Dover

Delaney a giant ripping out country lanes (de-lane-ing)

Evans vans shaped like the capital letter E, the spine of the letter being the top of the van

Farren a tiny little bird (wren) seen at a phenomenally far distance

Goddard God with a 'hard' expression on his face

Humphrey a delighted prisoner humming a happy song as he is let out from behind the bars

Ivy ivy

King a Memory Principle throne

Lawrence Arabia!

Mercer someone pleading for and being given mercy

Nunn nun

Ovett imagine a veterinary surgeon swinging in a gigantic O

Patterson imagine the pitter-patter of your own son or the son of a friend as his little feet scurry across the ground

Quarry a gigantic and strong-coloured open-land mining area

Richardson picture in your mind the son of a 'rich, hard' father

Scott develop a symbol, such as kilt, haggis; anything typical, for you, of a Scottish person

Taylor make a suitable image

Underwood make sure the wood under which you place the image of the person is memorable, such as an old giant fallen tree

Villars a magnificent gleaming white Mediterranean villa

Wade imagine a person/animal wading thigh-high through a lake

Xanthou a standardised Memory Principle Image of 'Thank you'

Young a springtime image

Zimmermann an image of someone 'zimming' (like skimming/zooming) across the surface of water

Using the Social Etiquette Method, the Mnemonic Method and your standardised name/image system, you will now be well on the way to becoming a master in the memorisation of names and faces.

One more magic ingredient can be added to your ability, and it is summarised in an event that changed my life and that largely initiated my own interest in the art and science of memory. The event took place in the first class on the first day of my first year at my university. It was an eight-in-the-morning English lecture, and even the excitement of this first day had not quite managed to shake off the sleepiness in some of our heads. Our lecturer did. He strode into the room with no briefcase, no writing materials, no notes and no books, stood in front of the class, announced his name, and then said he would call the roll. Standing in front of the podium with his hands behind his back, he started calling out our names in alphabetical order, going through Adams, Alexander, Barlow and Bossy, in response to which he got the usual mumbled 'yes, sir' and 'here, sir'. When he came to Camburn, however, there was no reply. He paused for a moment and then said, 'Mr Barry Camburn.' There was still no reply. Without change of expression, he then said: 'Mr Barry Camburn, address 29 West Street, phone number 272-7376, born 24 June 1943, father's name Frank, mother's name Mary.' The only reply he got was the widening eyeballs and opened mouths of everyone else in the class. Our lecturer continued calling the roll, and every time he arrived at the name of a person who was absent, he called out the person's Christian name, address, telephone number, date of birth, and parents' names.

It was obvious to us that he could in no way have forelearned who was absent, and therefore he must have *all* of that data on *all of us* totally memorised. When he had completed the roll and everyone was sitting amazed, he repeated very rapidly the names of the students who were absent and said, with a wry smile on his face, 'I'll make a note of that sometime.'

Though he had never seen any of us, he managed to remember our names and our personal data in perfect order.

Onword

Using the knowledge you gain from this book, see if you can work out how our lecturer accomplished this feat, and when you have worked it out, apply it.

16 _____   6 _____

12 _____

9 _____   19 _____

4 _____   15 _____

11 _____

18 _____   10 _____

3 _____   8 _____

14 _____

17 _____   7 _____

5 _____   2 _____

1 _____

20 _____   13 _____

Re-remembering –
Remembering What You Have Forgotten

24

The secret in re-remembering is to allow the full power of your memory to flow freely without 'trying' to remember any one specific thing.

I recently sat down to a relaxed and delightful dinner with some business associates who included the newly elected president of a training and development organisation. He announced at the beginning of the meal that he had to get something off his chest or he'd explode: his car had just been broken into, the windscreen smashed and his briefcase stolen. He was particularly frustrated because the briefcase contained his diary and a number of other items important to him.

As the pre-dinner drinks were downed, and the hors d'oeuvres completed, we began to notice that our friend was not really participating in the conversation and that he seemed to have a faraway look on his face as he very occasionally jotted notes on a scrap of paper. He eventually burst into the conversation again, announcing that he was ruining the evening for himself because he could remember only four items that had been contained in his stolen briefcase, that he knew there were many more, that he had to give a full report to the police within two hours, and that the more he tried to remember the more blocked he became.

Consider what you would have recommended that he do in order to recall.

Several of us at the table who were familiar with Memory Principles then took him through the following exercise: instead of continuing to allow him to concentrate on what he could not remember (what he in effect was doing was concentrating more and more on the *absence* of memory), we took him through what I call Reliving the Immediate Relevant Past. We asked him when he had last had his briefcase open. It turned out that it was at the office just before he left work, at which point he suddenly remembered that he had put two important magazine articles on the top of the pile in the briefcase. We then asked him when he had last had the briefcase open before leaving home for work. It turned out to have been the previous night after dinner, and he remembered having put in two more articles plus a tape recorder and a calculator, in preparation for the following morning. Finally we asked him to describe the interior design of his briefcase, and as he went through a detailed description of each compartment and section, he remembered pens, pencils, machines, letters and a number of other items that he had previously completely 'forgotten'.

Within 20 minutes of what turned out to be a delightful and playful reliving of his previous 24 hours, in which his frown gradually turned into a broad smile and his physical poise improved, he recalled 18 additional items to the original four he had recalled after a painful and unpleasant one hour and 20 minutes.

The secret is to 'forget about' whatever it is you are trying to remember and to surround the absence (what you have forgotten) with every possible association or connection available to you (see diagram below). Usually the best way to do this is to 'relive' all experiences that connect in any way with the item you are trying

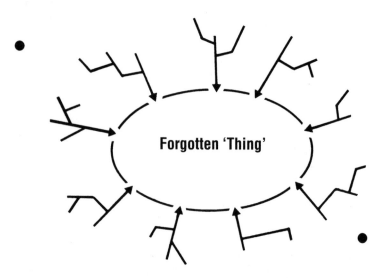

to remember. This technique works immediately in practically all cases, and basically takes the form of an internally or externally created Mind Map around the 'absent' centre.

In those rare instances where there is not an immediate recall, complete the reliving exercise in exactly the way outlined, and then give your brain the instruction to forget about it on the conscious level but work it out on an unconscious level. You will find that within a few hours or days of this 'programming' you will suddenly be taken by surprise at a meeting, while driving your car, in the shower, on going to sleep or waking, in the bathroom, etc., when your memory supplies the item you have forgotten.

Onword

This memory technique, like the others, improves all other aspects of your memory as well as your creativity, and in addition gives you a special boost of confidence when you realise that, no matter what you have forgotten, you have within the left and right hemispheres of your brain an unconscious Sherlock Holmes who will solve any memory mystery you choose to give him!

Remembering for Examinations

You need no longer fear examinations!

- No more the year-long dread that increasingly looms like a storm on the approaching horizon as the year progresses.
- No longer the frantic, rushed, sweaty, frightening final few weeks' and days' build-up of tension before the event.
- No longer the stressful dash into the examination room in order to save every available second.
- No longer the nervous first rush through the examination paper, during which you read so fast that you have to read it again to find out what is actually being asked.
- No longer will you need to spend as much as 15 to 30 minutes of a one-hour examination jotting down random notes, scratching your head, frowning, frantically trying to recall all that you know and yet at the moment for some reason seem not to remember.
- No longer the frustration of not being able to dig out the essence from the mire of your generally disorganised knowledge.
- No longer the horrible fear that the 'one dreaded question' may be there.
- No longer the feeling that the entire contents of your brain are leaving your head!

The common scenario suggested above applies not only to those who know little about the subject but often to those who have a great deal of knowledge. I remember at least three students in my undergraduate years who knew more about certain subjects than practically everyone else in the year and who consequently used to give private tutoring and coaching to those who were struggling. Extraordinarily, these bright students would regularly fail to excel at examination time, invariably complaining that they had not had enough time in the examination room to gather together the mass of knowledge that they had and that for some reason they 'forgot' at critical moments.

All these problems can be overcome by preparing for examinations using the techniques for reading and studying outlined in *Use Your Head* and *The Speed Reading Book*, applying the Mind Map memory techniques as outlined in chapter 22 and especially by using the Major System in conjunction with the Link System. Assume, for example, that the subject you wish to study and prepare to be examined in is psychology. As you study and organise your notes throughout the year, you would consciously and continually build up categories as demonstrated when remembering jokes (*see page 174*) that contain all the subcategories of the information.

In psychology these categories might include the following:

1 Major headings
2 Major theories
3 Important experiments
4 Significant lectures
5 Important books
6 Important papers
7 General significant points
8 Personal insights, thoughts and theories

Using the Major System you would allot a certain section to each of these major headings, attaching the Key Memory Image Words from your subjects to the appropriate Major System or Key Memory Image Word. For example, if you had devoted the numbers 30 to 50 to important psychological experiments, and the fifth of these was an experiment by the behavioural psychologist B. F. Skinner in which pigeons learned to peck for the reward of grain, you would imagine an enormous suit of armour (mail) taking the place of the skin (Skinner) of a giant and warriorlike pigeon who was pecking at the sun, causing millions of tons of grain to pour from heaven.

Using this approach, you will find it possible to contain an entire year's study within the numbers 1 to 100 and to transmit this organised and well-understood knowledge into flowing, first-class examination papers. If, for example, you were asked, in your psychology exam, to discuss motivation and learning with reference to behavioural psychology, you would pick the Key Words from the question and run them down your Major System Memory Matrix, pulling out any items that were in any way relevant to the question. Thus, the general form of your opening paragraph might be as follows:

In discussing the question of 'motivation and learning with reference to behavioural psychology', I wish to consider the following main areas of psychology: blank, blank, blank and blank; the following five theories: blank, blank, blank, blank and blank; the following three experiments, which support hypothesis A: blank, blank and blank; the following two experiments, which support hypothesis B: blank and blank; and the following five experiments, which support hypothesis C: blank, blank, blank, blank and blank.

In discussing the above, I wish to quote from the following books: blank, blank and blank; make reference to papers by blank, blank, blank, blank, blank and blank; include further references from course lectures given by blank on the following subjects: blank, blank, blank and blank; on the following dates: blank, blank, blank and blank.

And finally, in the conclusion of my answer, I will add a few of my own insights and thoughts in the following areas: blank, blank, blank and blank.

As you can see, you are already well on the way to a good grade, and at this stage you are still breezing through the introduction to your answer! It is worth emphasising that in any subject area the last category in your Memory System should be for your own creative and original ideas. It is in this category that the difference between first- and second-class examination results lies.

Brain Bites

For a comprehensive coverage of how to prepare, read and study for exams, read the chapters in *The Mind Map Book* and *Use Your Head* on the Mind Map Organic Study Technique (MMOST).

Onword

Besides being able to remember information perfectly for examinations, by using the systems outlined in this book, you will also be cultivating the creative powers of your mind that lead to your complete success.

Memory System for
Speeches, Jokes, Dramatic Parts, Poems, Articles and Books

Preview

- Speeches
- Jokes
- Dramatic Parts and Poems
- Articles
- Books
- Mind Map Method
- Poem Memory Exercise

The secret of making a good speech is not to remember the entire speech word for word, but the main Key Words of your speech.

Speeches

The best way to start approaching the memorisation of speeches is to realise that in 90 per cent of cases they do not need to be completely memorised. Realisation of this fact will instantaneously help you overcome most of the major problems experienced by those who approach speech writing and speech making as a memory function:

1   The enormous amount of time wasted in preparing a speech for memorisation. The average time taken for the preparation and presentation of a one-hour speech is, in

total, one week. This wasted time is spent writing and rewriting the speech again and again to make it appropriate for memorisation. The remainder of the wasted time is spent trying to ram the speech into the memory by constant repetition.

2 The mental pressure and stress caused.

3 The physical stress resulting from item 2.

4 The relatively stilted presentation that results from a word-for-word memorised presentation.

5 The boredom experienced by the audience who will 'sense' that what they are being given is lineally memorised and rigid, and not spontaneous and immediately relevant to them.

6 The aura of stress in both the speaker and the audience, both of whom wait with apprehension for those horrible gaps and pauses that occur when something has been forgotten.

7 The lack of eye contact between the speaker and the audience because the speaker is 'looking inward' at the rigidly memorised material and not outward to the audience.

The entire process of preparation and memory/presentation can be made both enjoyable and easy if you follow these simple steps:

1 ● Research
Generally **research** the topic about which you are going to speak, recording ideas. quotations and references you think will prove relevant. This should be done in the **Mind Map** form as basically outlined in chapter 22 and expanded upon in *The Mind Map Book* and *Use Your Head*.

2 ● Mind Map – Basic Structure
Having completed your basic research, sit down and plan out, using a **Mind Map**, the basic structure of your presentation.

3 ● Mind Map – Entire Speech
With your basic structure in front of you, fill in any important details, still in **Mind Map** form, so that you have completed a left- and right-brain, associative, imagistic Mind Map Memory Note of the **entire speech**. Usually this will contain no more than 100 words.

4 ● Practise

Practise making your speech from this completed outline. You will find that, as you **practise**, the final order in which you wish to present the speech will become increasingly clear, and you can number the main areas and subtitles of your speech appropriately. You will also find that, having completed the research and thought in this way about the structure of the material, you will already have automatically memorised the bulk of your speech. Initially, of course, there will be points in it at which you will hesitate or get lost, but with a little practice you will find that you not only know your speech from beginning to end but know, at a much deeper level than most speakers, the real associations, connections and deeper structures of your speech. In other words, you will *really* know what you are talking about. This point is especially important, for it means that when you finally do speak to your audience, you will have no fear of forgetting the word order of what you are presenting. You will simply say what you have to say smoothly, using the vocabulary appropriate for the moment and not getting bogged down in a rigid succession of preordained sentence structures. You will thus become a creative and dynamic speaker.

An excellent book for those who wish to explore the art of presentation more fully is *Present Yourself* by Michael J. Gelb. In his book, Gelb bases his entire theory and approach on the Principles and information presented in *Use Your Head* and *Use Your Memory*.

5 ● Peg Systems

As a backup safety system, you can always use one of the basic **Peg Systems**. Select the 10, 20 or 30 Key Words that completely summarise your speech and use the Memory Principles to connect your speech Key Words to the Peg System, thus guaranteeing that even if, for a moment, you do get lost, you will immediately be able to find yourself. Don't worry about any little pauses that might occur in your speech. When an audience senses that a speaker knows what he or she is talking about, a pause is actually more positive than negative, for it makes it obvious to the audience that the speaker is actually thinking and creating on the platform. This adds to the enjoyment of listening, for it makes the presentation far less formal and more personal and natural. Some great speakers actually use the pause as a technique, maintaining electrifying 'thinking silences' of up to as much as a full minute.

In those very rare instances when you do have to memorise an entire speech word for word, the process can be made easy by applying everything discussed so far in relation to speeches, and then, for the finishing touches, applying the techniques outlined in Dramatic Parts and Poems in this chapter.

Jokes

The problems and embarrassments associated with the memorisation and the telling of jokes are almost endless. In recent studies of business people and students, it was found that of the thousands of people questioned, nearly 80 per cent thought of themselves as not particularly good joke tellers, all wanted to be good joke tellers, and all listed memory as their major obstacle. The memorisation of jokes is actually far easier to deal with than the memorisation of speeches because the entire creative aspect of the work has already been done for you. The solution is in two parts: first, to establish a basic grid to categorise and capture the main element of the joke; and second, to remember the main details.

The first of these areas is easily dealt with by using a section of the Major System as a permanent library for the jokes you wish to file. First, divide the kind of jokes you wish to tell into general categories. For example:

Animal jokes
'Intellectual' jokes
Kids' jokes
National jokes (Irish, Japanese, etc.)
Rhyming jokes
'Saying' jokes
Sexual jokes
Sport jokes, etc.
Toilet jokes

List these in numerical preference order and then devote sections of your Major System to these categories. For example, you might have the area from 1 to 10 or 1 to 20 for sexual jokes, the numbers from 10 to 20 or 20 to 40 for national jokes, and so on.

The second area is equally easy to handle: once again it involves your use of the Link System. Let us take, for example, the joke about the man who went into a pub and bought a pint of beer. Having been given his beer, he suddenly realised he had to make an urgent phone call, but he knew that some of the characters in the pub would swipe his pint before he returned. In order to prevent this, he wrote on the glass, 'I am the world's karate champion,' and went to make his telephone call, securely thinking that his beer was safe. When he returned, he immediately saw that his glass was empty, and he noticed more scribbling underneath his own. It read: 'Thanks for the pint – the world's fastest runner!'

To remember the joke, you consciously select Major Key Words from it, joining them to form the basic narrative. All you need from this entire joke are the Key Memory Words: 'pint', 'phone', 'karate champion' and 'fastest runner'.

To complete your memorisation, you imaginatively link the first Key Word to the appropriate Key Word in the Major System, and you use the Link System to connect the remaining three Key Memory Words. There are two major advantages to using this system: first, you will be able to remember clearly and categorise whatever jokes you wish; and second, the mass involvement of your right brain in the memorisation of the joke itself will make you a far more creative and imaginative joke *teller*, thus overcoming the second major problem for jokers, that of getting in a too rigid and linear, left-brained memorisation mode, which bores the listener.

Dramatic Parts and Poems

For the university student, schoolchild and professional or amateur actor, this aspect of memory can be the most troublesome of all. The method usually recommended and employed is to read a line over and over again, 'get it'; read the next line, 'get it'; join the two together, 'get them'; read the next line and so on and so on ad nauseam until the first lines have been forgotten.

Systems based on the Memory Principles and used successfully by famous actors and actresses are the reverse. In this system the material to be remembered is read and reread quickly (see *The Speed Reading Book*) and with understanding over a period of four days, approximately five to ten times per day. If you read for understanding continually in this way, you will become far more familiar with the material than you realise at the end of the twentieth reading, and you will be able to recall, without looking at the text, most of the material to be remembered. Your mind, especially if you have used your right-brain imagination to help you understand, will have absorbed practically 90 per cent of the information, and remembering will have become a natural outgrowth of proper reading and basic understanding using the tools of imagination and association.

This system is far more successful than the line-by-line repetition system, and it can be improved upon even further in the following way: once again you use Key Memory Words and the Link System. For example, if the material to be remembered is poetry, a few Key Words will help your mind 'fill in' the remaining word-gaps. If the material to be remembered is part of a script, once again the Key Image Words and Link Systems prove essential. The basic subdivisions of a long speech can be strung together with Key-Word ease, and cues from speaker to speaker can be handled far more effectively if you imaginatively mnemonicise the quantum leap between the previous speaker's last word and your next word. It is lack of the use of these mnemonic techniques that often causes chaos on the stage, especially those long silences and breaks in continuity that occur when one performer forgets his last word or another forgets his first. Acting troupes can save as much as 50 per cent of their time, and thus enormously reduce stress and increase enjoyment and efficiency, by applying the Memory Principles to the theatrical works in which they are involved.

Articles

You may need to remember the content of articles on a short-term or long-term basis, and the systems for remembering each are different. If you have to attend a meeting or make a brief résumé of an article you have only recently read, you can remember it almost totally, and at the same time can astound your listeners, by remembering the pages to which you are referring. The method is simple: take one, two or three Key Memory Image Words from each page of the article and slot them on to one of your Peg Memory Systems. If there is only one Key Image Word per page, you will know that when you are down to Key Image Word number 5 in your system, you are referring to the fifth page of the article, whereas if there are two ideas per page and you are at Memory Word 7, you will know you are at the top of page four.

For the memorisation of an article over a long period of time, it will be necessary for you to choose more than two or three Key Image Words per page and to use a more permanent Peg System in conjunction with the review programme as outlined in chapter 11.

Books

It is possible to memorise, in detail, an entire book! You simply apply the memory techniques for articles to each page of the book you wish to remember. This is easily done using the Major and Link Systems in combination. Simply take one, two or three Key

Memory Image Words for page one and creatively link them to your Major System Memory Word for number 1: *day*. From page two you select another one, two or three Key Memory Image Words, creatively linking them to your number 2 Major System Key Memory Word: *Noah*, and so on. It will thus be possible for you, in a 300-page book, to remember not only what the basic content of each page was but, if you wish, what each section of each page contained.

Mind Map Method

The other particularly effective method for memorising an entire book, article, dramatic part or poem, is the Mind Map method. Each chapter or section of the material you wish to memorise can be a branch of your Mind Map. If this is imaged and coloured, your brain will remember both the image and the colour, *and* the *position* of the branch on the 'clockface' of the Mind Map. Because the Mind Map uses all of your cortical skills, the probability of overall and particular memory is dramatically increased, as is the probability that if something should be forgotten, all the surrounding information on the Mind Map will 'pop up' the momentarily forgotten information.

Poem Memory Exercise

Try your new skills on this poem by the author, SIMILE (ten minutes for perfection would be excellent):

Simile

What time does the universe say?
How constant is the sun?
How bright is the brightest day?
How ugly is blackest sin?
Who was earth's Joseph, who the ass, the God?
How noiseless is the circulation of the blood?
How short is the life of a wave?
What lithe youth bends with the wind?
How gentle and mild was rib-made Eve?
What concept frames the limit of the mind?
Where in curved space is Time's original spring?
How chaste is all the bee-sucked blossoming?

And what kind of butterflies grow from trains?

Catching
Your Dreams

27

Standard ability to remember dreams varies enormously from individual
to individual, but with the Memory Principles you have already learned,
everyone can tap into their subconscious.

Some people have such bad memories for their dreams that they
sincerely believe that they are non-dreamers. This is not the case,
for research during the past twenty years has shown that every
human being has regular periods throughout the night during
which dreaming takes place. This is evidenced by Rapid Eye
Movement, in which the eyelids flicker and flutter, and occasionally
the entire body twitches, as the body internally 'sees' and 'moves'
with the imaginary story. If you have a cat or a dog, you may have
noticed this kind of activity while it sleeps, for most higher
mammals also dream.

The first step in the memorisation of your dreams is the actual
retrieval of the dream itself. This you can accomplish by 'setting'
your mind just before you go to sleep. As you begin to drift off,
gently and firmly repeat to yourself 'I will remember my dream,
I will remember my dream, I will remember my dream.' This will
'programme' your brain to give priority when you awake to the
recall of the dream. It may take as many as three weeks before
you 'catch' your first one, but the process is infallible.

Once you have caught a dream, you enter the second stage of
dream memorisation. This is a tricky and 'dangerous' moment, for
if you become too excited by the fact that you have actually caught

one, you will lose it. This is because, for this type of memorisation, your brain needs to remain, for a while, in a *non-excited* state. You must learn to maintain an almost meditational calm, gently reviewing the main elements of the dream. You then very gently select two or three of the Key Main Images from the dream, and attach these, using the Memory Principles (which are dreamlike in themselves) through one of your basic Peg Systems.

Let's imagine, for example, that you had dreamed that you were an Eskimo stranded on an ice-floe at the North Pole and that you were writing, with gigantic felt-tipped pens, messages for help in the northern sky, forming multicoloured words that looked like the aurora borealis. For this you would need only two items from any Peg System. Take, for example, the Alphabet System. In this you would imagine that on the ice-floe with you was a gigantic and hairy *ape*, shivering exaggeratedly in the cold with you and thumping his chest to keep warm as an enormous *bee* buzzed in and out of the multicoloured images you were writing in the sky (see Colour Plate IV). Note that although the Alphabet System Image Word for the letter *A* suggested in chapter 9 is *ace*, it is permissible, as here, to use an alternative of your own choice.

Attaching the Major Dream Images to your Major Key Word System Memory Images in this way allows you to easily span the different brain-wave states in which you find yourself when asleep, when waking and when fully awake, thus enabling you to remember that important and very useful part of your subconscious life.

Numerous studies completed on people who have started to remember their dreams show that, over a period of months, they become more calm, more motivated, more colourful, more humorous, more imaginative, more creative, and far better able to remember. All of this is not surprising, for our unconscious dream world is a constant playground for the right side of the brain, where all of the Memory Principles are practised to perfection. Getting in touch with these at the conscious level encourages all connected skills to improve automatically.

If, as many people do, you become interested in this area of self-exploration and improvement, it is useful to keep a dream diary in Key Memory Word and Key Memory Image Mind Map form (see chapter 22). This diary will give you constant practice in all the skills mentioned and will become an increasingly useful tool in your overall self-development. After a little practice you may well find yourself both appreciating and creating literature and art at levels you had not previously explored.

Brain Bites

Edgar Allan Poe first remembered and then used the more nightmarish of his dreams as the basis for his short horror stories. Similarly, Salvador Dali, the surrealist artist, publicly stated that many of his paintings were reproductions of perfectly remembered images from his dreams.

It should now be clear to you that the development of memory skills not only gives you the advantage of being able to remember more than you used to but also encourages the total development of the left and right hemispheres of your brain. This leads to a general expansion of memory powers, a burgeoning of your ability to create, and consequently a similar burgeoning of your capacity to appreciate the arts and sciences. It also enables you to understand yourself and the major areas of knowledge far more easily, and to contribute creatively to the storehouse of human creativity and knowledge.

Conclusion and Exercises for the Future

Memory-Improvement Exercises

1 Start a programme of learning new subjects and new languages, in order to increase the basic memory store.

2 Encourage in yourself any activity that you have noticed helps you to remember.

3 Pay attention to your dreams, checking carefully the memory images which you thought you had 'previously forgotten'.

4 Occasionally attempt to 'take yourself back' to a period in your life, exploring *all* the elements of your life at that time.

5 Keep a diary using Key Words, special little drawings, as many colours as possible and Mind Maps.

6 Use the special Memory Systems and special Memory System Techniques for pleasure, for exercise, and for remembering.

7 Organise your learning time so that the primary and recency effects are maximised, and so that the sag-in-the-middle during learning is minimised.

8 Review, making sure that your review takes place just before the memory of what you want to remember starts to drop.

9 Encourage the use of your right cortical processes, as it is this side which provides you with the images and colour that make remembering easier.

10 Try to see and sense things in as much detail as possible – the more detail you store, the greater will be your ability to recall.

If you do this, and continue to remind yourself to remember by regularly referring to your books on memory, by leaving reminder notes in appropriate places, by devising review schedules and by asking other people to do 'spot checks' with you, your mind and memory will provide you with increasingly improved performance for the rest of your life.

Conclusion

Now that you have completed *Use Your Memory*, you have started a giant mental engine running that will serve you for the rest of your life.

The more you practise the Memory Foundations and Principles, the more powerful your memory will become. The more powerful your memory becomes, the more your creativity grows. The more your memory and creativity grow, the more astute and honed becomes each of your senses.

You have therefore initiated a positive spiral of personal growth and development that will enable you not only to remember your dreams, but to make them come true. When you apply the Principles outlined in *Use Your Memory*, your capacities will expand tremendously. Hopefully we will see you as a member of the Mnemons, and participating in the Student and/or World Memory Championships.

An increasing number of people are beginning to follow the same path, and for your reference pages 191–2 include information on Buzan courses, products and seminars that will assist you in pursuing any of your personal development goals.

To your good and cherished memories!

Bibliography

Aiken, E.G., Thomas, G.S., and **Shennum, W.A.** 'Memory for a lecture: Effects of notes, lecture rate, and information density.' *Journal of Educational Psychology* **67** (3), 439–44, 1975.

Anderson, J.R. *Cognitive Psychology and Its Implications.* Second edition. New York: W.H. Freeman & Co., 1985.

Anderson, J.R. 'Retrieval of propositional information from long-term memory.' *Cognitive Psychology* **6**, 451–74, 1974.

Anokhin, P.K. 'The Forming of Natural and Artificial intelligence.' *Impact of Science on Society*, Vol. XXIII **3**, 1973.

Ashcraft, M.H. *Human memory and cognition.* Glenview, Illinois: Scott, Foresman & Co., 1989.

Atkinson, Richard C., and **Shiffrin, Richard M.** 'The Control of Short-term Memory.' *Scientific American*, August 1971.

Baddeley, Alan D. *The Psychology of Memory.* New York: Harper & Row, 1976.

Bever, T., and **Chiarello, R.** 'Cerebral dominance in musicians and non-musicians.' *Science* **185**, 137–9, 1974.

Bloch, Michael. 'Improving Mental Performance' biographical notes. Los Angeles: Tel/Syn, 1990.

Borges, Jorge Luis. *Fictions* (especially 'Funes, the Memorious'). London: J. Calder, 1985.

Bourne, L.E., Jr., Dominowski, R.L., Loftus, E.F., and **Healy, A.F.** *Cognitive Processes.* Englewood Cliffs, NJ: Prentice-Hall Inc., 1986.

Bower, G.H., and **Hilgard, E.R.** *Theories of Learning.* Englewood Cliffs, NJ: Prentice-Hall Inc., 1981.

Bower, G.H., Clark, M.C., Lesgold, A.M., and **Winzenz, D.** 'Hierarchical retrieval schemes in recall of categorized word lists.' *Journal of Verbal Learning and Verbal Behavior* **8**, 323–43, 1969.

Breznitz, Z. 'Reducing the gap in reading performance between Israeli lower- and middle-class first-grade pupils.' *Journal of Psychology* **121** (5), 491–501, 1988.

Brown, Mark. *Memory Matters.* Newton Abbot: David & Charles, 1977.

Brown, R., and **McNeil, D.** 'The "Tip-of-the-Tongue" Phenomenon.' *Journal of Verbal Learning and Verbal Behavior* **5**, 325–37.

Bugelski, B.R., Kidd, E., and **Segmen, J.** 'Image as a mediator in one-trial paired-associate learning.' *Journal of Experimental Psychology* **76**, 69–73, 1968.

Buzan, Tony. The Mind Set: *Use Your Head, Master your Memory, The Mind Map Book* and *The Speed Reading Book.* All London: BBC Worldwide, 2000.

Buzan, Tony. *W H Smith GCSE Revision Guides* (60)

Buzan, Tony. *Head First, The Power of Creative Intelligence, The Power of Spiritual Intelligence, The Power of Social Intelligence, The Power of Verbal Intelligence, Head Strong, How to Mind Map.* All London: Harper Collins, 2002.

Carew, T.J., Hawkins, R.D., and **Kandel, E.R.** 'Differential classical conditioning of a defensive withdrawal reflex in Aplysia Californica.' *Science* **219**, 397–400, 1983.

Catron, R.M., and **Wingenbach, N.** 'Developing the potential of the gifted reader.' *Theory into Practice*, **25** (2), 134–140, 1986.

Cooper, L.A., and **Shepard, R.N.** 'Chronometric studies of the rotation of mental images.' In Chase, W.G. (Ed.) *Visual Information Processing*. New York: Academic Press, 1973.

Daehler, M.W., and **Bukatko, D.** *Cognitive Development*. New York: Alfred A. Knopf, 1985.

Domjan, M. and **Burkhard, B.** *The Principles of Learning and Behavior*. Monterey, Cal.: Brooks/Cole Publishing Co., 1982.

Dryden, Gordon and **Vos, Jeanette** (Ed.). *The Learning Revolution*. Sacramento, Cal.: Jalmar Press, 1993.

Edwards, B. *Drawing on the Right Side of the Brain*. Los Angeles: J.P. Tarcher, 1979.

Eich, J., Weingartner, H., Stillman, R.C., and **Gillin, J.C.** 'State-dependent accessibility of retrieval cues in the retention of a categorized list.' *Journal of Verbal Learning and Verbal Behaviour* **14**, 408–17, 1975.

Erickson, T.C. 'Spread of epileptic discharge.' *Archives of Neurology and Psychiatry* **43**, 429–452, 1940.

Fantino, E., and **Logan, C.A.** *The Experimental Analysis of Behavior: A Biological Perspective*. San Francisco: W. H. Freeman & Co., 1979.

Frase, L.T., and **Schwartz, B.J.** 'Effect of question production and answering on prose recall.' *Journal of Educational Psychology* **67** (5), 628–35, 1975.

Freidman, A., and **Polson, M.** 'Hemispheres as independent resource systems: Limited-capacity processing and cerebral specialisation.' *Journal of Experimental Psychology: Human Perception and Performance* **7**, 1031–58, 1981.

Gawain, S. *Creative Visualization*. Toronto: Bantam Books, 1978.

Gazzaniga, M. 'Right hemisphere language following brain bisection: A 20-year perspective.' *American Psychologist* **38** (5), 525–37, 1983.

Gazzaniga, M. *Mind Matters*. Boston: Houghton Mifflin Co., 1988.

Gazzaniga, M. *The Social Brain*. New York: Basic Books Inc., 1985.

Gazzaniga, M. and **DeDoux, J.E.** *The Integrated Mind*. New York: Plenum Press, 1978.

Gelb, Michael J. *How to Think Like Leonardo da Vinci*. New York: Delacorte Press, 1998.

Gelb, Michael J., and **Buzan, Tony.** *Lessons from the Art of Juggling*. New York: Harmony Books, 1994.

Glass, A.L., and **Holyoak, K.J.** *Cognition*. New York: Random House,1986.

Godden, D.R., and **Baddeley, A.D.** 'Context-dependent memory in two natural environments: On land and under water.' *British Journal of Psychology* **66**, 325–31, 1975.

Good, T.L., and **Brophy, J.E.** *Educational Psychology*. New York: Holt, Rinehart and Winston, 1980.

Greene, R.L. 'A common basis for recency effects in immediate and delayed recall.' *Journal of Experimental Psychology: Learning, Memory and Cognition* **12** (3), 413–18, 1986.

Greenfield, Susan. *Brainpower: Working Out the Human*. Element Books, 2000.

Greenfield, Susan. *Human Brain: A Guided Tour*. London: Phoenix, 2000.

Grof, S. *Beyond the Brain: Birth, Death, and Transcendence in Psychotherapy*. New York: State University of New York Press, 1985.

Haber, Ralph N. 'How We Remember What We See.' *Scientific American*, 105, May 1970.

Halpern, D.F. *Thought and Knowledge: An Introduction to Critical Thinking*. Hillsdale, NJ: Erlbaum, 1984.

Hampton-Turner, C. *Maps of the Mind*. New York: Collier Books, 1981.

Hearst, E. *The First Century of Experimental Psychology.* Hillsdale, NJ: Lawrence Erlbaum Associates, 1979.

Hellige, J. 'Interhemispheric interaction: Models, paradigms and recent findings., In D. Ottoson (Ed.) *Duality and unity of the brain: Unified functioning and specialization of the hemispheres.* London: Macmillan Press Ltd, 1987.

Hirst, W. 'Improving Memory.' In M. Gazzaniga (Ed.) *Perspectives in memory research.* Cambridge, Mass.: The MIT Press, 1988.

Hooper, J., and **Teresi, D.** *The Three-pound Universe.* New York: Dell Publishing Co. Inc., 1986.

Howe, M.J.A. 'Using Students' Notes to Examine the Role of the Individual Learner in Acquiring Meaningful Subject Matter.' *Journal of Educational Research* **64**, 61–3.

Hunt, E., and **Love, T.** 'How Good Can Memory Be?' In A.W. Melton and E. Martin (Eds.) *Coding Processes in Human Memory,* Washington, DC: Winston, Wiley, 1972, op.

Hunter, I.M.L. 'An Exceptional Memory.' *British Journal of Psychology* **68**, 155–64, 1977.

Kandel, E.R., and **Schwartz, J.H.** 'Molecular biology of learning: Modulation of transmitter release.' *Science* **218**, 433–43, 1982.

Keyes, Daniel. *The Minds of Billy Milligan.* New York: Random House, 1981; London: Bantam, 1982.

Kimble, D.P. *Biological Psychology.* New York: Holt, Rinehart and Winston Inc., 1988.

Kinsbourne, M., and **Cook, J.** 'Generalized and lateralized effects of concurrent verbalization on a unimanual skill.' *Quarterly Journal of Experimental Psychology* **23**, 341–5, 1971.

Korn, E.R. 'The use of altered states of consciousness and imagery in physical and pain rehabilitation.' *Journal of Mental Imagery* **7** (1), 25–34, 1983.

Kosslyn, S.M. *Ghosts in the Mind's Machine.* New York: W.W. Norton & Co., 1983.

Kosslyn, S.M. 'Imagery in Learning.' In M. Gazzaniga (Ed.) *Perspectives in Memory Research.* Cambridge, Mass.: The MIT Press, 1988.

Kosslyn, S.M., Ball, R.M., and **Reiser, B.J.** 'Visual images preserve metric spatial information: Evidence from studies of image scanning.' *Journal of Experimental Psychology: Human Perception and Performance* **4**, 47–60, 1978.

Kotulak, Ronald. *Inside the Brain.* Andrews McMeel Publishing, 1997.

LaBerge, S. *Lucid Dreaming.* New York: Ballantine Books, 1985.

LaPorte, R.E., and **Nath, R.** 'Role of performance goals in prose learning.' *Journal of Educational Psychology* **68**, 260–4, 1976.

Leeds, R., Wedner, E., and **Bloch, B.** *What to say when: A guide to more effective communication.* Dubuque, Iowa: Wm. C. Brown Co. Publishers, 1988.

Loftus, E.F. *Eyewitness Testimony.* Cambridge, Mass.: Harvard University Press, 1980.

Loftus, E.F., and **Zanni, G.** 'Eyewitness testimony: The influence of wording of a question.' *Bulletin of the Psychonomic Society* **5**, 86–8, 1975.

Luria, A.R. *The Mind of a Mnemonist.* London: Jonathan Cape, 1969.

Madigan, S.A. 'Interserial repetition and coding processes in free recall.' *Journal of Verbal Learning and Verbal Behavior* **8**, 828–35, 1969.

Matlin, W.M. *Cognition.* New York: Holt, Rinehart & Winston Inc., 1989.

Mayer, R.E. *Thinking, problem solving, cognition.* New York: W. H. Freeman & Co., 1983.

Mendak, P.A. 'Reading and the Art of Guessing.' *Reading World* **22** (4), 346–51, May 1983.

Miller, G.A. 'The magical number seven, plus or minus two: Some limits on our capacity for processing information.' *Psychological Review* **63**, 81–97, 1956.

Miller, W.H. *Reading Diagnosis Kit.* West Nyack, NY: The Centre for Applied Research in Education, 1978.

Neisser, U. *Memory Observed: Remembering in Natural Contexts.* San Francisco: W.H. Freeman & Co., 1982.

Nelson, T.O. 'Savings and forgetting from long-term memory.' *Journal of Verbal Learning and Verbal Behavior* **10**, 568–76, 1971.

North,Vanda. *Get Ahead.* UK: Buzan Centres Ltd, 1993.

Ornstein, R. *The Psychology of Consciousness.* New York: Harcourt Brace Jovanovich, 1977.

Paivio, A. 'Effects of imagery instructions and concreteness of memory pegs in a mnemonic system,' *Proceedings of the 76th Annual Convention of the American Psychological Association,* 77–8, 1968.

Paivio, A. *Imagery and Verbal Processes.* New York: Holt, Rinehart & Winston Inc., 1971.

Penfield, W., and **Perot, P.** 'The Brain's Record of Auditory and Visual Experience: A Final Summary and Discussion.' *Brain* **86**, 595–702.

Penfield, W., and **Roberts, L.** *Speech and Brain-Mechanisms.* Princeton, NJ: Princeton University Press, 1959.

Penry, J. *Looking at Faces and Remembering Them: A Guide to Facial Identification.* London: Elek Books, 1971, op.

Recht, D.R. and **Leslie, L.** 'Effect of prior knowledge on good and poor readers' memory of text.' *Journal of Educational Psychology* **80** (1),16–20, 1988.

Reid, G. 'Accelerated learning: Technical training can be fun.' *Training and Development Journal* **39** (9), 24–7, 1985.

Reystak, R.M. *The Mind.* Toronto: Bantam Books, 1988.

Rickards, J.P., and **DiVesta, F.J.** *Journal of Educational Psychology* **66** (3), 354–62, 1974.

Robertson-Tchabo, E.A., **Hausman, C.P.,** and **Arenberg, D.** 'A classical mnemonic for older learners: A trip that works!' In K.W. Schaie and J. Geiwitz (Eds.) *Adult development and aging.* Boston: Little, Brown & Co, 1982.

Robinson, A.D. 'What you see is what you get.' *Training and Development Journal* **38** (5), 34–9, 1984.

Rogers, T.B., Kuiper, N.A., and **Kirker, W.S.** 'Self-reference and the encoding of personal information.' *Journal of Personality and Social Psychology* **35**, 677–88, 1977.

Rosenfield, I. *The Invention of Memory: A New View of the Brain.* New York: Basic Books Inc., 1988.

Rossi, E.L. *The Psychobiology of Mind-Body Healing: New Concepts of Therapeutic Hypnosis.* New York: W.W. Norton & Co., 1986.

Ruger, H.A., and **Bussenius, C.E.** *Memory.* New York: Teachers College Press, 1913, op.

Russell, Peter. *The Brain Book.* London: Routledge & Kegan Paul, 1966; Ark, 1984.

Schachter, S., and **Singer, J.E.** 'Cognitive, social and physiological determinants of emotional state.' *Psychological Review* **69**, 377–99, 1962.

Schaie, K.W., and **Geiwitz, J.** *Adult Development and Aging.* Boston: Little, Brown & Co., 1982.

Siegel, B.S. *Love, Medicine and Miracles.* New York: Harper & Row,1986.

Skinner, B.F. *The Behavior of Organisms; An Experimental Analysis.* New York: Appleton-Century-Crofts, 1938.

Snyder, S.H. *Drugs and the Brain.* New York: W.H. Freeman & Co., 1986.

Sperling, G.A. 'The information available in brief visual presentation.' *Psychological Monographs* **74**, Whole No. 498, 1960.

Sperry, R.W. 'Hemispheric deconnection and unity in conscious awareness.' *Scientific American* **23**, 723–33, 1968.

Springer, S., and **Deutch, G.** *Left Brain, Right Brain.* New York: W. H. Freeman & Co., 1985.

Standing, Lionel. 'Learning 10,000 Pictures.' *Quarterly Journal of Experimental Psychology* **25**, 207–22.

Stratton, George M. 'The Mnemonic Feat of the "Shass Pollak".' *Physiological Review* **24**, 244–7.

Suzuki, S. *Nurtured by love: a new approach to education.* New York: Exposition Press, 1969.

Tart, C.T. *Altered States of Consciousness.* New York: John Wiley & Sons Inc. 1969.

Thomas, E.J. 'The Variation of Memory with Time for Information Appearing During a Lecture.' *Studies in Adult Education*, 57–62, April 1972.

Toffler, A. *Power Shift: knowledge, wealth and violence in the twenty first century.* London: Bantam Books, 1992.

Tulving, E. 'The Effects of Presentation and Recall of Materials in Free-Recall Learning.' *Journal of Verbal Learning and Verbal Behaviour* **6**, 175–84.

Van Wagenen, W., and **Herren, R.** 'Surgical division of commissural pathways in the corpus callosum.' *Archives of Neurology and Psychiatry* **44**, 740–59, 1940.

von Restorff, H. 'Über die Wirkung von Bereichsbildungen im Spurenfeld.' *Psychologische Forschung* **18**, 299–342.

Wagner, D. 'Memories of Morocco: the influence of age, schooling and environment on memory.' *Cognitive Psychology* **10**, 1–28, 1978.

Walsh, D.A. 'Age difference in learning and memory.' In D.S. Woodruff and J.E. Birren (Eds.) *Aging: Scientific perspectives and Social Issues.* Monterey, Cal: Brooks/Cole Publishing Co., 1975.

Warren, R.M., and **Warren, R.P.** 'Auditory illusions and confusions.' *Scientific American* **223**, 30–6, 1970.

Wolford, G. 'Function of distinct associations for paired-associate performance.' *Psychological Review* **73**, 303–13, 1971.

Yates, F.A. *The Art of Memory.* London: Routledge & Kegan Paul, 1966; Ark, 1984.

Zaidel, E. 'A response to Gazzaniga: Language in the right hemisphere: Convergent perspectives.' *American Psychologist* **38** (5), 542–6, 1983.

Index

BUZAN CENTRES

Learning and Thinking
for the 21st century

We are dedicated to creating a Mentally Literate Planet –
a world where people know how to learn and think

DEVELOP YOUR INTELLECTUAL CAPITAL

with customised seminars designed to improve performance

In-Company training
Licensing for companies and independent trainers
'Open' Business Seminars
Educational Seminars

We are the ONLY organisation that can license use of the
Mind Maps® and associated trademarks

FOR FULL DETAILS OF

BUZAN LEARNING SEMINARS

and information on our range of brain-friendly products including:

- books
- software
- audio and video tapes
- support materials

SEND FOR OUR BROCHURE

Contact us at:

Buzan Centres Ltd (UK and Rest of World)
54 Parkstone Road
Poole, Dorset, BH15 2PG
Telephone: 44 (0) 1202 674676
Fax: 44 (0) 1202 674776
Email: buzan@buzancentres.com
Website: www.Mind-Map.com

Buzan Centres Inc (Americas)
PO Box 4,Palm Beach
Florida, 33480, USA
Telephone: 001 561 881 0188
Toll free: 001 866 896 1024
Email: buzan@buzancentres.com
Website: www.Mind-Map.com

THE BRAIN TRUST CHARITY, #1001012 – invites your contribution
to assist brain research into effective processes for the enhancement of
learning, thinking and the potential of all.